to explore! —*Auntie Mame* First of all, move m... light my eyes. —*Denis Diderot* I'm looking for the suggestion ...e see eventually the completely apparent takes a moment from running away. —*Eudora Welty* I have come to ...y work and my life through memory. —*Gloria Vanderbilt* ...on. —*Henri Cartier-Bresson* The question is not what you look at, ...e art of perceiving similarity among disparate things. ...Lennon Genius is only a superior power of seeing. —*John Ruskin* ...s. —*Lau Tzu* . . . First to look, and then to observe and ...n the world only new arrangements of things, ...gs you will know. The more things you learn, the more ...mage, no more. —*Gerard De Nerval* The power, and usefulness, of ...uch with the themes of one's own life that is the ...re with you. —*Gloria Vanderbilt* There's only one thing in life and that's ...nd And I'll bury my soul in a scrapbook, with ...o keep going. You must never stop. It's the only way of life I ...ession, you produce the best of the best. —*Madeleine Castaing* ...eking new landscapes but in having new eyes. —*Marcel Proust* ...*Minamoto No Sanetomo* I don't want to be reasonable there's plenty ...ation, foolishness and discovery. —*Mirabel Osler*

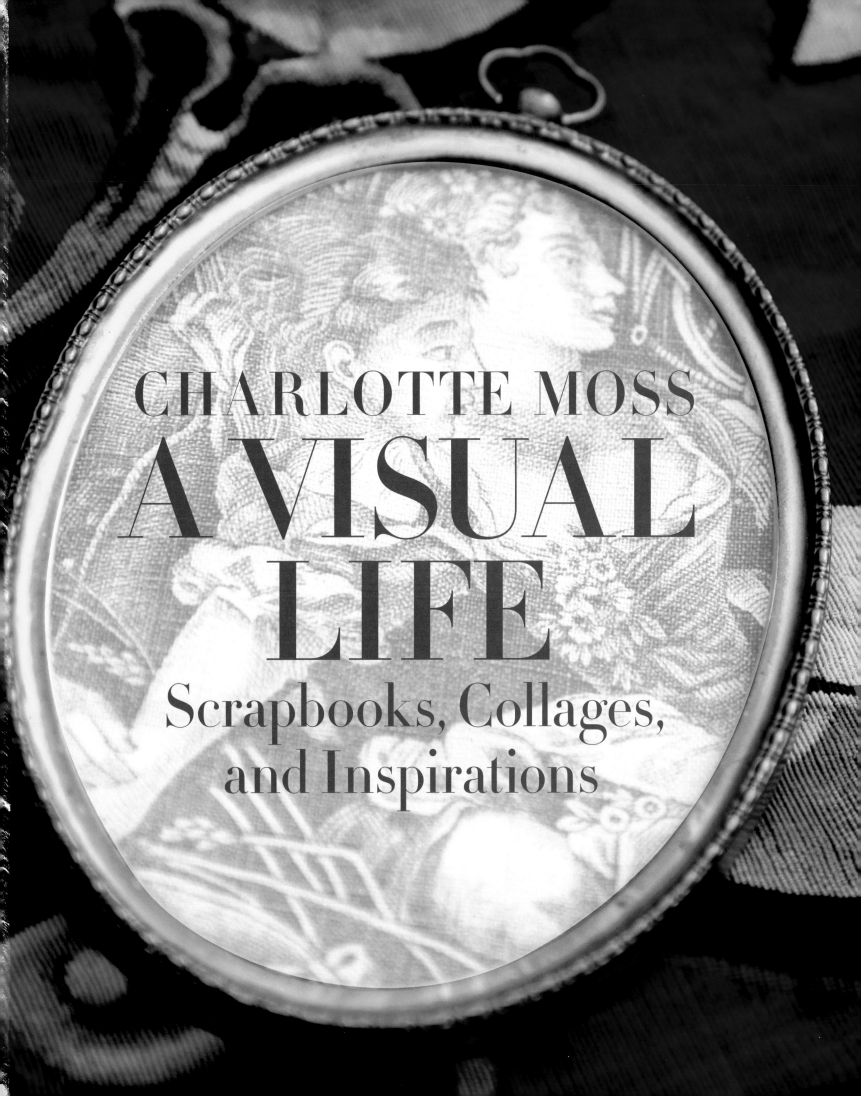

CHARLOTTE MOSS
A VISUAL LIFE

Scrapbooks, Collages, and Inspirations

CHARLOTTE MOSS
A VISUAL LIFE

Scrapbooks, Collages, and Inspirations

RIZZOLI
NEW YORK

New York · Paris · London · Milan

L'oie de la Forêt
de la Reine
Sa Compotée de chou rouge
et chataignes de Bitche

CONTENTS

6
CUT & PASTE
Curating Inspiration

32
Obsessed with Recording
Candy Pratts Price

37
IT'S MY PLEASURE

74
Infinite Variety
Deeda Blair

76
A HOME IS
AN AUTOBIOGRAPHY

128
My Visual Instruction
Alexa Hampton

130
LITTLE PLEASURES

178
Scrapbooking in the Digital Age
Deborah Needleman

181
BEYOND THE HORIZON

228
Beyond the Horizon
Pamela Fiori

232
THE HOUSE IN MY HEAD

266
CONTRIBUTORS
RESOURCES
ACKNOWLEDGMENTS
CREDITS

Beauty

Let me see a female possessing the beauty of a meek
and modest deportment — of an eye that bespeaks intelligence and purity within — of the life that
speaks no guile; let me see in her a kind benevolent disposition, a heart that can sympathize with
distress, and I will ...
that dwells in ...
on the snowy hand
which our poets have
fade when touched
these ever ...
will outlive the
brighter and ...
roll away.

Good Wishes
To Mrs P Porter

Sweet as fragrance of the morn
When Nature's all in bloom —
When flowers the hills and ...
With golden hues at noon.
Sweet as Autumn ... which
On dipped in golden dyes
Sweet as the moon with silver
Walks in the peaceful skies
Sweet as the bowers of heaven ...
High up on Zions hill;
Where saints and angels — heaven
Their holy Temples fill.
Sweet as the hymns of angels
Along the Plains above

To Miss P. Damon.

... thine — the joy that springs
young; untainted bosoms;
begins to plunge her wings;
... spreads her first sweet ...
... thine — the purer bliss,
... hearts is given;

ARTICLES

GARDENS

OBJECTS

ROOMS

COLLAGE

ART

CURATING INSPIRATION

Making things by hand has always come naturally to me. I grew up around women who created: my grandmother embroidered and gardened; my mother always had a project in her hand. She cross-stitched, knitted my father's sweaters, canned vegetables and relishes, made Christmas ornaments, and more.

I have always collected things, wherever I go, whether they were shells, objects, ideas, quotes, or images taken by my camera. It was natural that I would be drawn to collage. As I am a visually inspired person, collage has been my vehicle for recording and retaining important moments in my life, as well as absorbing things that I am drawn to: still-lifes, gardens, interiors, and fashion among them. The medium welcomes chance findings and randomness and understands the consequence might well be a totally unintended one. These collages, put into books, have become my treasured visual memoirs, personal storyboards, my inspiration, and my creative outlet for years--the DNA of my design aesthetic as well as the story of my life so far. And I'm more aware than ever about the importance of these hand-recorded memories and dreams for my family and for the future.

"There are no new ideas in the world, only new arrangements of things," Henri Cartier-Bresson once said, and I will add that I believe one must know what came before to rearrange in a new way, to contribute something fresh today. My friend Pamela Fiori says that unless you have a reference for history, the Wailing Wall would just be a wall, and I agree wholeheartedly. In my life I've been inspired by strong women throughout history. I've studied their lives and taken bits and pieces from each, collecting them in my own personal handbook of women who had a flair for living and lived it with flair. Some of these thoughts and visuals have been physically collected and collaged in my scrapbooks--working documents that have been essential in my evolution as a designer. I'm a teacher in my work. I am always studying and learning. By examining what others have written and done and processing those ideas with my hands, scissors, and a glue stick, I've been able to develop my own approach to living and design, one that works for my home and my life--the basis of which has been honed from others over the course of my career

AN EDITING LIFE Putting order to our thoughts-- *OH*, let me count the ways. It can be through words organized in the form of diaries or journals, or capturing images through thoughtful photography. I believe recording memories is important in order to capture the emotion, the fervor, and the meaning of the moment.

As a young married woman in the '70s, I was reinvigorated after college to work with my hands. Everyone was doing crafts; we were reacting to the sterile, plastic-filled world spawned by the '60s. Gloria Vanderbilt had just written a book on collage, telling us of "the power, and usefulness, of collage as a way of thinking, of getting in touch with the themes of one's own life." I accelerated my needlepoint, which now had a purpose: it's what I decorated with in my earliest homes. Soon my collaging had a purpose, too. When I started a career in design, I used collage to distill my thoughts by gathering a variety of images into one picture that could give clients an idea of what I'd envisioned for their homes. When I traveled, I accumulated ideas and artifacts from my trips and turned to collage as a way to capture these inspirations, observations, and insights. These personal storyboards became my way of processing visual information. So when I took my nieces to Paris and came home with several digital memory cards full with--well, just that--memories, I began organizing them in collage, for them and for me. I want to be able to look back on that trip and remember every moment. I could not do that without my scrapbooks.

One year, a gift arrived from my niece Charlotte; this accordion collage in a decorated box. I didn't know how bad she had caught the bug. I smiled. It must be in the genes.

Collage always made sense for me as a methodology. I am a forager, a hunter, a gatherer, a collector, an editor--in truth, a stylist, I think, since birth. I see the world in composition--always have. A gathering of anything, anywhere, inside or out, can be arranged into a still life: smooth stones gathered during a walk on the beach fill bowls or cluster beneath a bust in my East Hampton home. In New York, stacks of antique fabrics in a cabinet are topped with gilt-wood fragments or an enormous antique tassel. I've learned that the most ordinary of found objects artfully considered and arranged can be elevated. And it's in these created environments that we share a specific point of view, a personal aesthetic, a vision, and a passion for life. In essence, creating a composition is about seeing. And sometimes, it's seeing the beauty in ordinary, everyday found objects. I took a photograph of maple leaves in an early morning frost and placed it in one of my gardening scrapbooks; it always reminds me of the incredible, understated power of simplicity. I'm drawn to compositions of tablescapes and arrangements that have an air of effortlessness. I love that found, imperfect, *wabi-sabi* beauty. I have studied the ease in others' arrangements and digested them in the hopes of assimilating the same ease into my work.

While compositions may be about seeing, they also speak volumes about who we are. We tell stories every day--in the way we put ourselves together in the morning, in how we furnish our rooms, and in the photos we take. Take, for example, a charm bracelet: a collection of items, mini ornaments, each special, signifying some place or someone. My collection of bracelets serves that purpose; each holds a memory for me, and depending on how they're put together, they can make a variety of

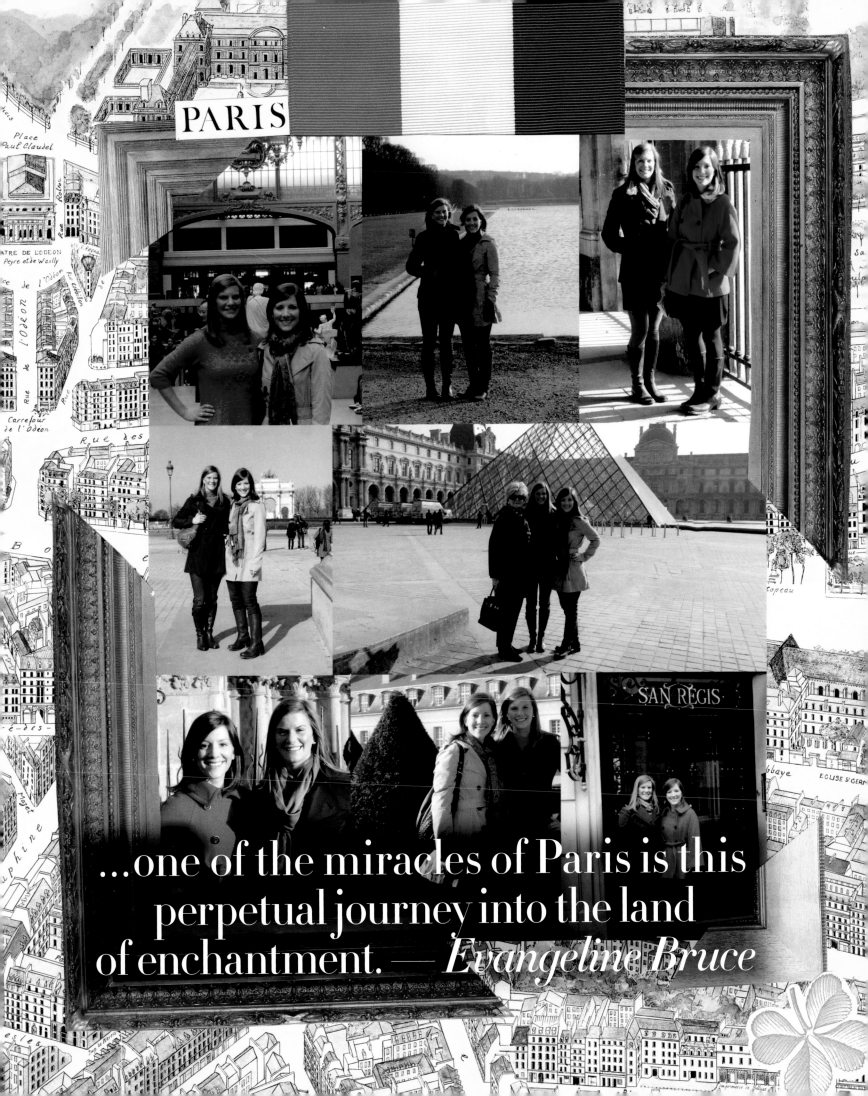

PARIS

...one of the miracles of Paris is this perpetual journey into the land of enchantment. — *Evangeline Bruce*

different statements. How we decorate, the things we buy along the way, and the objects that speak to us--the self is sublimated and made visible in the inanimate. Our collections become metaphors for our lives. Our belongings speak for us even before we've opened our mouths.

"Found objects, chance creations . . . abolish the separation between art and life. The commonplace is miraculous if rightly seen, if recognized," wrote poet Charles Simic. How true. Collage is a vehicle for disseminating ideas, organizing thoughts, and developing and determining your tastes. What I most appreciate about collage is that it's not a snob. It's an art form for everyman; it is ignorant of skill level and thoroughly forgiving. Collage doesn't require a deft hand like painting, yet it has been prevalent in fine art though the ages. Collage has seen us through cubism, surrealism, constructivism, and abstract expressionism. Artists throughout history have embraced the technique, artists such as Braque, Picasso, Jasper Johns, and so many others. Collage became a twentieth-century art form thanks to these artists. Dreams, dissonance, eccentric and disparate bits and pieces merged to produce juxtapositions that gave the subconscious and our inspirations a legitimate outlet. Unrelated elements--all the better, dig deeper and metaphors often surface. Collage permits experimentation. It legitimizes childishness and playfulness--perhaps one of the key factors in its popularity, and why there are millions of people creating collages in their scrapbooks and supporting a multimillion-dollar industry today.

Today, blogs have become digital forms of collage. Many bloggers act as curators, taking a bit from here, an inspiration from there--defining their aesthetic by synthesizing and putting looks together on the screen. Often they're even Photoshopping those inspirations into mood boards. We can see what our friends are inspired by on their Pinterest boards or Twitter streams; both are collages of ideas. The Internet, our 24-hour news cycle, and our various handheld devices all contribute

to the overabundance of information in our lives. Through all that, collage has become a vital tool in helping us organize and disseminate what is important to us.

Vogue.com creative director Candy Pratts Price is an absolute whirling dervish scrapbooker. As she is someone who heads up the fashion bible's digital presence, I've enjoyed learning of her absolute love of collecting her life's fabulous memories and turning them into art in her many scrapbooks. Candy bridges the digital and print worlds, as she even has books filled with CDs of video segments.

Just as websites and blogs use collage to convey themes, many photographers, Deborah Turbeville, Tim Walker, and Todd Selby, to name a few, and print publications continue to use the technique in a variety of ways. Newell Turner's Letter from the Editor in *House Beautiful* is a classic example and one of my monthly favorites. It stops you, engages you, and invites you into his world. *The New York Times Style Magazine*, *T*, always uses a collage of snapshots for its Profile in Style column; *Vogue* has employed the title "Scrapbook" for a column recently; and *Vanity Fair* and *In Style* regularly incorporate collage in recurring sections.

Although I am rarely without my iPad and iPhone, the fact remains that I am a diehard glue-stick-and-scissors kind of person. There's something intensely gratifying about working out ideas with your hands. Collage for me is a way to physically gather my inspirations and organize them, so I may refer back and remember what caught my eye--whether it's a breathtaking garden I photographed in Provence or a striking tablescape I tore out of *Maison & Decoration* magazine. Notepads are strategically placed all over my house for this purpose--on the bedside table, in the commode in the library, in the secretary in the living room. In the dining room, I even have a special green leather box shaped like a book that holds notecards for that moment when I get an idea during dinner, so I don't have to leave the table. A notebook and my Canon camera are always in my bag. It's unpredictable and often

totally random when those bits and pieces might come
together and create something that sparks a connection
that leads to an idea, a concept--something concrete.
Samantha Cameron (British prime minister David
Cameron's wife) aptly said, "Notebooks are to dreams
what computers are to reality." In my life, I have a
healthy dose of both.

The boxes that house my clippings and paper
fragments are like patient friends. We go through periods of calm
and relative inactivity. Moderate movement occurs when additions are being made
after having been accumulated in a traveling file, and the inevitable process
of editing takes place. Next, there is the organizing frenzy--paper pandemonium--
when I am preparing to work as I dissect material to see what is in abundance
and/or short supply. All collecting has its dry spells and its motherload
moments. But then the moment: the hours you have been waiting for, that period
of relative chaos, like a visit with a friend you haven't seen in a spell, and
the conversation is nonstop--so goes the collage. One piece leads to the next.
Oh yes, that one. No, this one--and this one next--and that--and that and--
that one will never quite do. It happens just so and every once in a while
someone draws a breath. A reunion.

When I start a travel scrapbook, my process usually begins the moment I pull the memory card out of my Canon Mark II or one of my smaller digital cameras. Each day of my trip I edit the day's photos in the cameras I've been using. I also keep a notebook in which I record thorough details about each location. When I return from a trip, I print thumbnails, review them, edit, and create a CD that's dated and labeled. The thumbnails and the disc then go into the photo archive. Next, I select which I want to put into the scrapbook, print them, and bundle them with ribbon and a tag indicating the name of the trip. Those bundles go into boxes until I have time to commit them to the page. The travel albums are mostly filled with collages of photos, yet sometimes it's a menu signed by the chef in a particularly memorable restaurant, or a receipt, business card, or clipping that's included. Relevant, important, or simply sentimental, it becomes my visual memory.

The process starts with building pages in my working scrapbooks: eleven-by-fourteen-inch, four-ring binders with page inserts of heavy, archival paper covered with acid-free Mylar sheet protectors. I work in these books until a story is complete, then I transfer them to a four-ring book in caramel leather made for me by the Vogel Bindery, including a title, such as "Provence 2012" or "East Hampton Gardens Summer 2011," and my initials embossed in gold. For the places I've been to again and again—France, England, Italy—I continue to add new pages after each visit. I never grow tired of photographing the light in Paris' Luxembourg Gardens or Palais-Royal. Each time something new presents itself.

My travel scrapbooks are predominantly filled with photographs, as are my garden notebooks, boxes, and scrapbooks, but other categories have different elements. Scrapbooks composed of my dinner parties include place cards and menu cards done by Rory Kotin of Scribe, Ink, a calligraphist, who has been doing mine for years. I will include a picture of the table setting and flowers, and the seating chart, which is handwritten on a table chart.

Then there are those books that document memorable life experiences. There are scrapbooks filled with photos of beautiful things, objects, and still lifes: *La dolce vita*, "Italy-in-the-'60s" style and fashion in general. Inspirational flower arrangements by others that have caught my eye; and "the house in my head," a title borrowed from Dorothy Rogers. I pull from my collections of old magazines from the '30s to the '70s: *Harpers Bazaar*, *House & Garden*, *Vogue*, *Town & Country*, and others. I tear from new magazines, too. Everything gets sorted by category. Then when it is quiet in the evening, while unwinding, listening to music or a TEDTalk on my iPad, I spread out a file and begin piecing things together. For me, collage is a process that can take on a life of its own. What starts out as one thing oftentimes ends up something else entirely--the spontaneity, the random and arbitrary placement of bits, pieces, fragments, seemingly disparate, but not. Every last piece is the result of saving, sifting, snipping in a process that can take hours or years to come together in a complete thought.

Sometimes I wonder, "Why did it take so long to get to this point?" A commitment to pieces and their locations, the accumulation can take years. Some items have been in my boxes for ten to fifteen years. Sometimes, leisurely sifting through, you edit and refine your collection. Editing is a creative process itself. Whatever the venture--editing your closet, your library, pruning your garden--it is all editing. All require clarity of thought, some creative vision, a sense of purpose, and dogged determination. Once completed, however, a sigh of relief, a glorious shoulder-dropping sigh of relief. What collage, blogging, and scrapbooking have in common is that they're all done to please the creator; the aggregation of thoughts, ideas, inspirations materialize into a new entity. You must be willing to let go and let instinct take over.

So why do we do it? The same could be asked of travel, reading fiction, or writing in a diary. Pleasure, I assume, but also to travel outside ourselves, to stretch ourselves and learn--to explore new terrritory in search of knowledge, insights, and satisfying curiosities.

Scrapbooking has been used by creative minds throughout history: Cecil Beaton, Christian Lacroix, Baron de Cabrol, Ralph Rucci, Frédéric Fekkai, Tim Walker, Richard Meier, Anna Dello Russo, and so many more. In fact, that is another very rich book altogether. In the last several years I have acquired material from four ladies: Elsie de Wolfe, Jacqueline Kennedy Onassis, Pauline Trigère, and Evangeline Bruce.

Elsie de Wolfe's personal scrapbook appeared at auction at Christie's in Los Angeles along with a number of other items. Bound in pink moiré silk, with the word "me" handwritten on the cover, it's the album Elsie put together about herself--the only album of its kind, offering a peek inside the life of the influential, early twentieth-century interior designer. And what an insightful album it is, filled with formal portraits, photos by Baron de Meyer and others, including quirky snapshots taken by

For the famed Italian couturier, grandeur is a working element, as **Georgina Howell** discovers

POSSESSED BY PAPER

I have this thing with paper. I am obsessed with the allure of paper and stationery. The colors, the texture, the sound of a fountain pen scratching across the surface. As a school child, I loved the double-ruled sort used for penmanship lessons even with a menacing nun presiding over the class. I loved to write, so I tried not to let her nervous jingling of rosary beads inhibit me. It was not easy.

The color and feel of brown paper bags at the supermarket caught my eye early on. Shades of camel, tobacco, chestnut, and whiskey are all derivatives of paper-bag-brown and are often used to describe the palette of my wardrobe. An attraction to one thing infuses itself into another.

I have found myself saving the packaging of candy from a beautiful Italian apothecary or a soap in a French hotel. Hotel stationery, gift tags, postcards, magazines, pages from antique books that have long since lost their covers, vintage wallpapers, a divine portfolio of antique marbled papers—the first purchase early one morning in the Paris flea market—all have their own place in my hierarchy of paper.

Everything Fleur does is a constant surprise. Years ago, I saw her walking out on the lawn overlooking the bay at our country house on Long Island. It was a beautiful day; there were sailboats on the water and the sky was the most lovely blue. Fleur had a piece of beaverboard and a palette of paints. She sat on a beach chair and gazed into space. When she came in later, we were all anxious to see her picture. She had painted a jungle scene with a leopard.

—*Eleanor Lambert*

friends—all of which reveal Elsie's personality, a work of *moi*.

Notes of Jackie Kennedy Onassis appeared in an auction catalogue for a Christmastime sale at Sotheby's. The material, once owned by a housekeeper, consists of many of Jackie's handwritten notes to the staff. Poring through these notes, mostly written on yellow legal pads, her paper of choice, I learned that Jacqueline Kennedy Onassis was a great manager. She had a benevolent way of telling people what they did and didn't do right. One note simply reads: "The Sanka was awful, the soufflé was perfect." She had handwritten a vitamin chart for her children. There are notes describing the contents of picnic lunches approved for their sojourns in Hyannis Port. These notes subtly unveil her management skills. She showed great finesse in dealing with and caring for people. A wonderful mother, a good manager, and a brilliant First Lady.

Kinsey Marable, an antique book dealer and someone who helps others collect and build a library, contacted me about Evangeline Bruce's decorating scrapbooks and notebooks. The renowned author and Washington hostess's scrapbooks include some pages of great French houses from various magazines and collages of Polaroids documenting the contents of her own house and what she liked in her friend's homes—the ultimate compliment.

One of fashion designer Paulene Trigère's entertaining notebooks came my way via a dealer who knew I would be interested. A small, red book: a collection of table-seating charts and menus, likely during the '70s. With a red (her favorite color) felt-tip pen, she recorded all of the ingredients to her dinner parties: who was there, what was on the menu, and little notes. One such note reads: "Fresh peony looks beautiful, party slow to start, everyone left at 2 a.m. I wore the old red dress." Her signature red linen dress boxes, her red bedroom, her red ink in a red book: I find joy in these precise selections. Once Fleur Cowles, upon my

for

Charlotte

with warm thoughts

Fleur Cowles

14/11/2006

request for her most sage piece of advice, without hesitation replied, "Select, select, select." And indeed she did.

Glimpsing into the lives of these women--through their hands, eyes, and ideas--has cemented my feelings about the importance of scrapbooking as an art, a historical document and, of course, a personal and creative outlet. It's a way to embrace the artist in ourselves by using the medium of very personal material, our own ideas, thoughts, and photographs, as well as those of others that inspire us. These treasured memoir books are your personal history. When I lecture, women often ask me how I find the time and how I organize myself enough to scrapbook. I tell them that what's important is just getting started. The best time to start is *now*. Create a system that works for you. When you make something beautiful, you will feel good about it. Then that energy, the exhilaration from having created something that you'll enjoy for years will give you the motivation to go back and tackle any material that has built up over time, piece by piece. Don't overreach. Know yourself and start slowly. Those stolen moments are most gratifying when you are organized to begin.

"Memory gives time elasticity," Clare Booth Luce said. "The happy time is short as it passes, but there is all of life in which to look back upon it." This is especially true if you've compiled those memories with your own hand into a memory book uniquely yours, whether aided by technology or scissors. Your own cut and paste.

THE GARDEN IN JUNE

THE GARDEN IN AUGUST

GARDEN IN AUTUMN

SUMMER HARVEST All summer long
I "harvest" the lemon verbena from my garden and dry
it in flat baskets. My summer crop provides infusions
for teas and dinner parties all winter for me and
my friends.

Pestos are made with the basils--Genovese, Greek,
and Thai are abundant all summer long. Parsley is
combined with pistachio to make another variation.
Fusilli, linguini, garganelli--a winter of options.

POSSIBILITIES

Scraps, fragments, clippings, fabric swatches, leaves, ribbons, photos, menus, tickets, stamps . . . I am a Miss Havisham of sorts. I have always been a collector. I see possibilities in things--found objects. It can take years later for some of it to make sense, to connect a thought--a project, a design, a concept, or simply a key image in a collage--like a jigsaw puzzle that sits waiting for someone to return and complete the picture. What's the rush? The joy is in the doing.

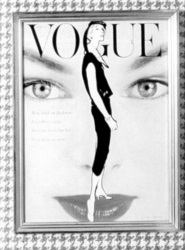

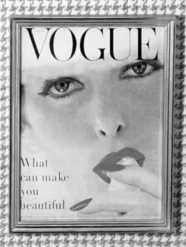

These covers were selected with a client for her powder room. *Je ne sais quoi . . .*
that's what these cover girls have in common. Together they make a powerful composition,
a collage of chic.

Presence, clean elegant lines, and simplicity with exuberance. This collection of images, from one of my scrapbooks on fashion, spans a period of over fifty years.

SUBJECT: OBSESSED WITH RECORDING
TO: Charlotte Moss
FROM: Candy Pratts Price

MEMO:

I learned scrapbooking at my mother's knee. I remember my mother and aunts assembling wonderful books of photographs secured by little black stick-on corners. They recorded every occasion—birthdays, baptisms, graduations, and weddings. They kept Christmas photos, and if there was wrapping paper they liked, they saved it, too. It's one of my earliest memories—seeing my mother and her sisters clip and mount their cherished things into albums.

Later, when I was traveling to the fashion collections for *Vogue* or *Bazaar*, the invitations to shows or private parties in Paris or Milan were what compelled me to start saving "stuff." Outstanding, over-the-top, and fabulous—the invitations were often calligraphed on beautiful heavy-stock paper with gold edging and embossed logos. At the time, I loved the fax machine (and I still love to fax); I was absolutely the back-to-back fax girl. Marc Jacobs sent me bags of faxes, as did friend and colleague André Leon Talley. I wanted to save the faxes (and the invites), so I would bring them home, arrange them the same way I might dress a window, and paste them in a book. Thumbing through the pages, I could relive the moment of that dinner, that party, or that fashion extravaganza. Just by keeping the invitation to John Galliano's show, for example, I could immediately recall its theme and his mood—insights invaluable for my work. And it was all so glamorous: I was staying at the Ritz in Paris, or jetting to India for Bloomingdale's, receiving all these incredible invitations, memos, and faxes. I knew I was a lucky girl; I wanted to freeze those moments, so I could look back and say, "Look at that! That's when I had that hairstyle," or "Those were my shoes!" or "Wasn't that a tender note from Steve" (my dear friend and late fashion designer Stephen Sprouse). Never was the intention for someone else to see these private pages.

Some of my scrapbooks are CDs onto which I've recorded Candycasts (a Vogue.com avatar of me talking fashion) and videoclips from when I've won an award. CD cases, in a way, are a modern version of scrapbooking. The ideal scrapbook is spiral-bound, so it can be laid flat on which to work. (But, between us, I never chose that route.) One of mine has a Chantilly lace cover and a small book fastened with black velvet ribbon. Another is a gorgeous yellow leather scrapbook from Asprey with vellum pages that I filled with photos, clippings, walks, and menus. Sometimes I'd use the scrapbook as a

guest book and invite visitors to draw in it. Then I began to buy my books from T. Anthony—beautiful, leather-bound books that were handcrafted and hand-stitched. Later, I ordered identical red-silk-covered books to be made for me in Paris at the superb artist supplies gallery Magasin Sennelier. As you can see, I have a library of scrapbooks.

When my husband Chuck (artist Charles Price) and I started building a house in Water Mill in Southampton, I put together one really huge scrapbook. It contains every single drawing that Chuck did for the house—every dream and wish that floats up when you start to design your *first* house. I was obsessed with recording the process. Into the scrapbook went clippings culled from magazines of household items or home-furnishing accessories I craved: a sink like this; hot water faucets for the bathroom that look like this; or, wouldn't a wall like the one at MoMA be great? Much of the inspiration for the house came from these saved product shots, and that scrapbook is a chronicle of how we built it. You can imagine how important it is to me.

My technique? First I put items into a bin or basket. Then I sort through the accumulation and edit. (It's so important to edit.) What seemed at one moment like, "Wow!" suddenly turns into "What's this?" Beyond the paper collectibles in the basket, there might be a piece of satin ribbon or other embellishment that I like, and I'll save it to gussy up a page. Next I gather my tools. I have a pair of Maped Créa Cut scissors with five interchangeable blades for varying trim patterns, and I have Precision Sandkaulen pinking shears made in Germany. For mounting, I use an OIC Precision Glue Stick because it's clear and acid free. At hand, I keep a batch of Magic Markers, a few colored paper clips, and a roll of tape. Lastly, I have a little red can of Best-Test rubber cement that I love because it doesn't shrink or wrinkle paper. Now, ta-dah! It's time to begin.

The design of my layouts evolves from a mood and the desire to build a story, so while the entries in a particular book might not seem logical or chronological, taken together they have a theme and a beginning, middle, and end. Were you to riffle through my books, you would find lots about Chuck and me and our anniversaries, shots of our dogs or other people's dogs, and tons of drawings, notes, invitations, photographs, and images from the fashion world.

One of the "parties and special events" books includes an engraved invitation from the Cartier International Polo match at Windsor Great Park and a stunning invitation from King Hussein of Jordan to Queen Rania's fortieth birthday party. There's also an invitation to a private sale of photos, drawings, and other memorabilia from the Diana Vreeland collection. Pride of place goes to an invitation to President Obama's inauguration.

I value personal notes or drawings. I have a cartoon from Gahan Wilson; the invitation to Kate Moss's wedding; cards from Giorgio Armani, Claude Montana, Vera Wang, and a handwritten note from Louboutin scrawled inside the sketch of a shoe. I have missives from Christian Lacroix and Christian Dior, Chanel and Givenchy, Calvin, Carolina, and Ralph. They all mean so much to me, but among my favorites are sketches of dresses my dear friend Stephen Sprouse designed for me. And who could resist the divine "Welcome to Paris" notes from Karl or the songs written to me along with thousands of cards from Marc (enough to warrant a book of its own) with funny, affectionate notes to "My dearest Muneca."

Drawings especially take you back. Giambattista Valli might send me a sketch for the Met party (the fabulous Metropolitan Museum of Art annual Costume Institute gala) with a note suggesting, "You should look like this. You should do this with your makeup." I save every element of the process—the illustration, the fabric swatches, the personal conversation that took place on paper. These mementoes are treasures for me. I love to browse through the books, revisiting those moments. And because fashion can be so fickle, it's great to be able to look back and see just how much my hand was in this industry.

Part of being able to fit this hobby into my life is that I'm up very early, usually at five thirty in the morning. It's a great private time to take care of certain things—file, arrange, read mail, edit, go through my closet. Scrapbooking is such a relaxing and enjoyable pastime. The process is yours. The work is yours. It's like a child at play, except you're an adult.

My advice for people who want to do scrapbooks: get started. Keep a calendar and pencil in your appointments and events. Then make a scrapbook of things that relate. Say you've gone to a flea market and bought a chair for ten dollars—paste in the receipt; if you've dined at a new restaurant— take a matchbook as a keepsake; or, you're excited about a new venture—save the business card of your contact and fasten it to a page. Invitations to parties, Playbills, wedding programs, a book jacket from a novel you loved: all these are grist for your scrapbook mill. Sometimes I use my iPhone to take a shot of my TV screen, usually an image of a great dress I see or a set design I like, then I print it out and preserve it. Anything goes!

I save days. That's what scrapbooking does. It allows you to save the days of your life.

CANDY PRATTS PRICE

The mellowing influence of good food on civilized beings cannot be underrated, or its importance exaggerated. It is conducive to success and, which is more important, to happiness. —*Elsa Maxwell* After a good dinner, one can forgive anybody, even one's own family. —*Oscar Wilde* Good tables are indeed the centers of happy homes, the lure and the sustainer of loving hearts. —*Savarin* Life is meals. —*James and Kay Salter* I made a menu book. I listed first courses, main courses, and all the sweets. I did it for lunch, dinner, teas, high teas, suppers before the theater, Christmas dinner. I would tell my cook, 'Any of these things suit me if you serve them just as I've written it down.' —*Nancy Lancaster* Plates should be hot, hot, hot; glasses cold, cold, cold; and decorations low, low, low. —*Elsie de Wolfe* A great hostess and creator of a salon needs an unflagging curiosity about other people. —*John Lehmann* A hostess needs to be bossy, to control conversation and mobilize friendships by shifting people around the room, preferably in so subtle a manner that her guests do not realized they are being manipulated; and she must ruthlessly exclude all bores from her table . . . —*Brian Masters* "It is not easy to define the quality by which one makes others feel friendly and happy at the very outset of a party, so that they, in their turn, can contribute to the general pleasure rather than count the time till it is not impolite to go home. I believe in some degree it is this quality of warmth, and if you can infuse this into the reception and care of everyone of your guests—even the unexpected ones—you will do well." —*Rosemary Hume*

FAY CE QUE VOUDRAS

FAY CE QUE VOUDRAS I once saw this medieval French expression carved in stone above a door in France. The perfect location for "do as you will," the portal that greets us and our invited guests everyday.

"Do what you will" is the same message I have about entertaining. Gone are the days when we only sit down to tables where everything is in the same finish--silver--and everything is the same material--bone china. Experiment with found objects, the unusual or most unlikely materials, create still-life centerpieces with what you own, combine old and new, and change your plates with each course.

Fay Ce Que Voudras, peel back the fear, throw away the rule book and make your own.

Return romanticism to the dinner table. Make your dinners "events." Romantics see the adventure in everyday life; a routine bores them. Romantics are opportunists; they love any chance to stretch their imaginations. Romantics believe in decorating for delight. Is there another reason?

Fay Ce Que Voudras. WHY NOT?

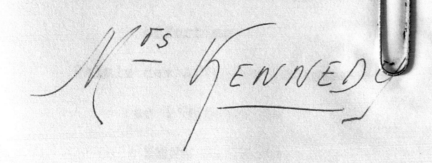

On February 14, 1962, First Lady Jacqueline Kennedy gave
America a valentine, a valentine that endures today and
will continue to endure for generations to come. Mrs.
Kennedy and Charles Collingwood of CBS (see photo on
page 47) walked fifty-six million Americans through the
newly refurbished White House. It was the first ever
televised tour of the presidential mansion by a First
Lady. There has not been a tour of its magnitude since.
Mrs. Kennedy wore a red bouclé suit by Chez Ninon, a model
of a Marc Bohan for Christian Dior. The shape, the fit, the
detail--are what we all refer to as iconic "Jackie style."

The project she
spearheaded, with the
support of the Fine
Arts Committee, was an
enormous undertaking
that required
planning, networking,
fund-raising, arm
twisting, and chutzpah.
She was thirty-one
when she took on the
project, the third
youngest First Lady
at that time, and a
young mother.

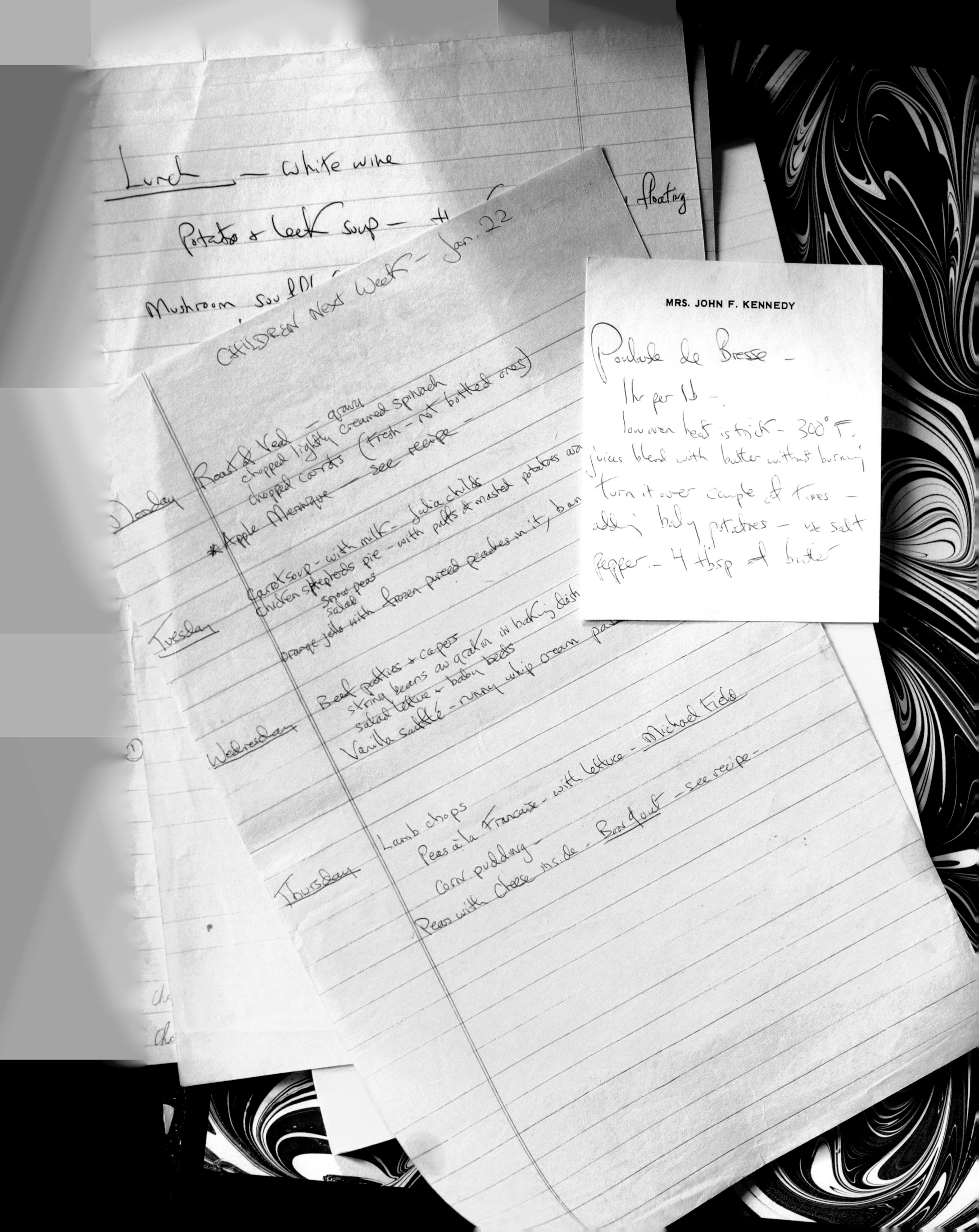

<u>Lunch</u> — White wine

Potato & Leek soup — H ...

Mushroom soup? DI... ... floating

CHILDREN Next Week — Jan. 22

Monday — Roast of Veal — gravy
chopped lightly creamed spinach
chopped carrots (fresh — not bottled ones)
*Apple Meringue — see recipe —

Tuesday — Carrot soup — with milk — Julia Childs
Chicken shepherds pie — with puffs of mashed potatoes around
snow peas
salad
Orange jello with frozen pureed peaches with ban...

Wednesday — Beef patties & capers
string beans au gratin in baking dish
salad lettuce & baby beets
Vanilla soufflé — runny whip cream pas...

Thursday — Lamb chops
Peas à la Francaise — with lettuce — Michael Field
Corn pudding —
Pears with cheese inside — Bon Jour — see recipe —

ch...

cho...

Poularde de Bresse —
1 hr per lb —
low oven heat is trick — 300° F.
juices blend with butter without burning
turn it over couple of times —
adding baby potatoes — use salt
pepper. — 4 tbsp of butter

With the help of Henry Dupont, Jayne Wrightsman, Rachel Lambert Mellon, and others, paintings, furniture, decorative objects, and cash began to find their way into the coffers of Mrs. Kennedy's storage rooms. Her dream was to make Americans proud of THEIR house, making it a true expression of American history, the American presidency, and the American people for everyone that passes through its doors, from foreign leaders to schoolchildren. Her desire for authenticity, accuracy, scholarship, and a tasteful and beautiful national home for all Americans made the White House what it is today.

Some years ago, a 500-page catalog announced what *Vogue* called the "sale of the century." Over four days some 1,200 lots of furniture, jewelry, books, antiquities, and art of the late Jacqueline Bouvier Kennedy Onassis were sold at Sotheby's. Hammer prices were record-breaking as expected by unfathomable margins, no matter the object, mundane, household, art, or beautiful jewelry.

Years later, and very quietly, several items slipped into another sale. I learned about them by chance, exercising one morning on the treadmill. I catch up on a lot of reading, magazines, auction catalogs, etc., and this time I spotted a watercolor by Mrs. Onassis. . . then another. . . then another lot had a description of notes written by her, notes to her staff, notes about how to feed the children, a vitamin chart, and menus. I read on. With the exception of the typed White House menus, all of the notes were in her hand on legal paper, her style of memos written about home--at home with a love of home. A few pages are shown here.

Saturday
Nov. 11, 1961

90 guests

DINNER

FOR: Princess Radziwill

Vol au Vent d'ecrevisse a la Nantua

Almaden
Grenache Rosa   Canard a l'orange

Riz Sauvage

Petits Pois a la Francaise

Mousse de Jambon au Porto

Salade Mimosa

Piper Heidsieck   Soupe Anglaise
1953

Demi-tasse

Salted Nuts   Mints & Chocolates

Wednesday
April 11, 1962

Number: 90

8:00 PM   DINNER

Shah of Iran

La Truite en chaud froid Doria

Guinea Hen Santa Clara
Wild Rice
Asperges Sauce Mousseline

Mousse de Foie Gras Dans sa Gelee
Rubis au Porto

Bombe Glacee Rustique

Mignardises Assorties

Chevalier Montrachet 1958

Chateau Haut Brion   1957

Moet et Chandon   1955

Sunday
April 29, 1962

DINNER

Nobel Prize Winners

La Couronne de l'elu Victoria

Filet de Boeuf Wellington

Pommes Chipp
Fonds d'artichauts Favorite
Endive Meuniere

Bombe Caribienne
Petits Fours Assortis

Puligny Montrachet Combetter ier Cru 1959

Chateau Mouton Rothschild 1955

Piper Heidsieck 1955

Tuesday
Nov. 27, 1962

BIRTHDAY PARTY

Creamed Chicken in Patty Shells

Green Peas

Carrot Sticks

Milk

Gumdrops

Vanilla Ice Cream (small scoops)
Chocolate Sauce
Strawberry Sauce

Two Birthday Cakes
(Caroline - Pink)
(John, Jr. Blue)

Mrs. Kennedy, a very young First Lady, as described by J. B. West, the Chief Usher of the White House, is included below. I have always found his description of her in these early days in the White House to be incredibly warm, caring, and respectful.

Jacqueline Kennedy whispered. Or so I thought, at first. Actually, she spoke so softly that one was forced to listen intently, forced to focus on her face and respond to her direct, compelling eyes . . . When she looked around a crowded room as if searching for the nearest exit, people assumed that she was shy, uncertain. I don't think she was ever shy. It was merely her method of studying the situation: memorizing the room, or assessing the people in it. She spoke no small talk . . . She limited her conversations merely to what, in her opinion, mattered. Her interests were wide, however, as was her knowledge, and she had a subtle, ingenious way of getting things accomplished . . . In public, she was elegant, aloof, dignified, and regal. In private, she was casual, impish, and irreverent. She had a will of iron, with more determination than anyone I have

ever met. Yet she was so soft-spoken, so deft and subtle,
that she could impose that will upon people without their
ever knowing it. Her wit--teasing, exaggerating, poking fun
at everything, including herself--was a surprise and a daily
delight . . . She had a total mastery of detail--endless,
endless detail--and she was highly organized, yet rarely
held herself to a schedule. For others, she insisted upon
order; for herself, she preferred spontaneity. She took
advice readily, but only when she asked for it, and she
strongly resisted being pushed . . . I saw her move swiftly
into three different roles: wife and mother to her young
children; commander-in-chief of the White House restoration;
and chatelaine of the Great Hall. -J.B. West

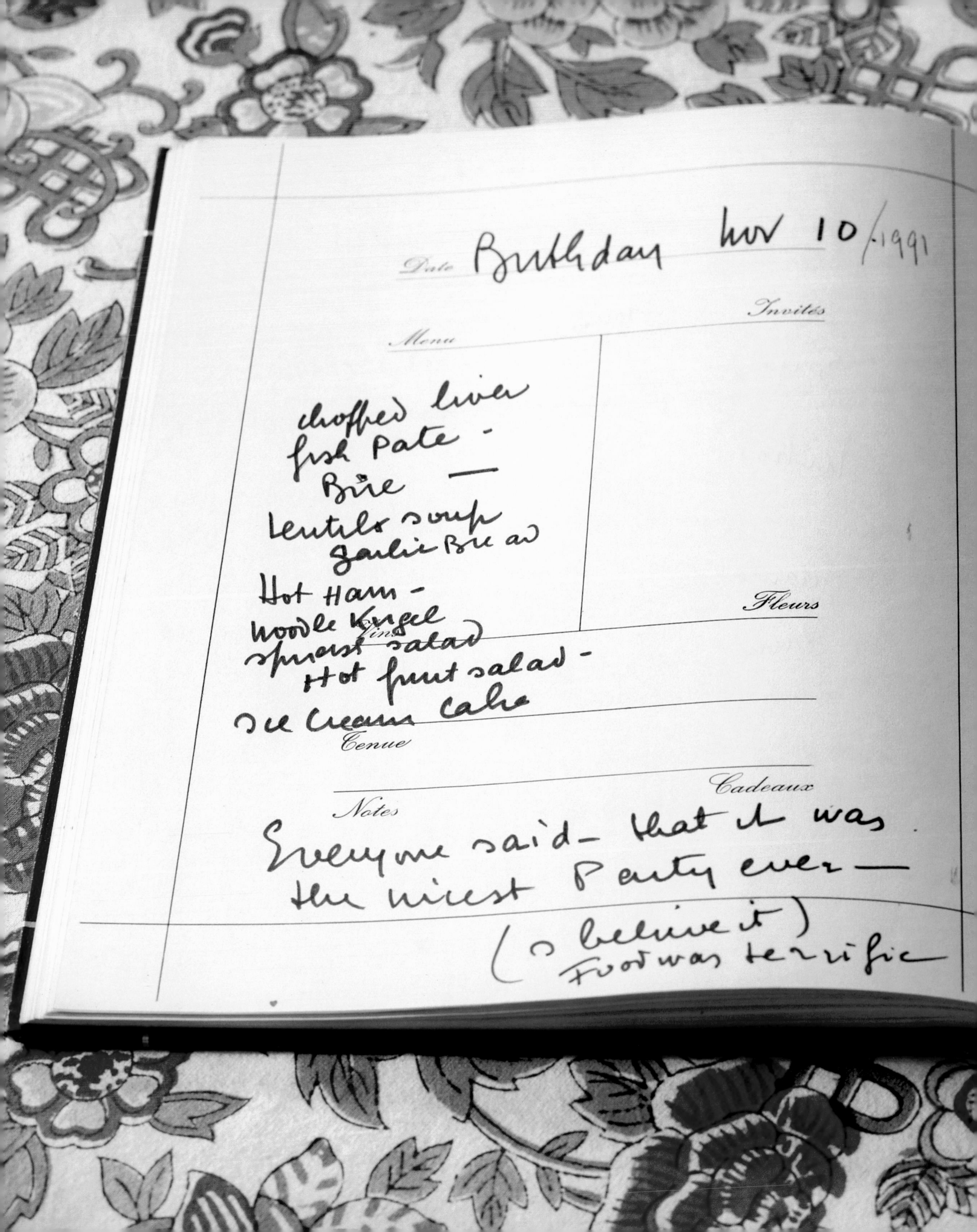

Date Birthday Nov 10/1991

Menu

Invités

chopped liver
fish Pate -
    Brie —
Lentils soup
    garlic Bread
Hot Ham -
noodle Kugel
spinach salad
    Hot fruit salad -
Ice Cream Cake

Fleurs

Tenue

Notes

Cadeaux

Everyone said— that it was
the nicest Party ever—

(o believe it)
Food was terrific

With a career that spanned over fifty years and a life of ninety-three, it is perhaps
not by coincidence that Pauline Trigère chose the turtle, the Chinese symbol for
longevity, as a key motif in her work. She had a collection of hundreds of turtles
in various forms. The name of her country house was *LA TORTUE*. Reportedly, for each
collection she designed a turtle print, like the scarf framing her here--a gift to
me from a dear vintage dealer.

paulinetrigère

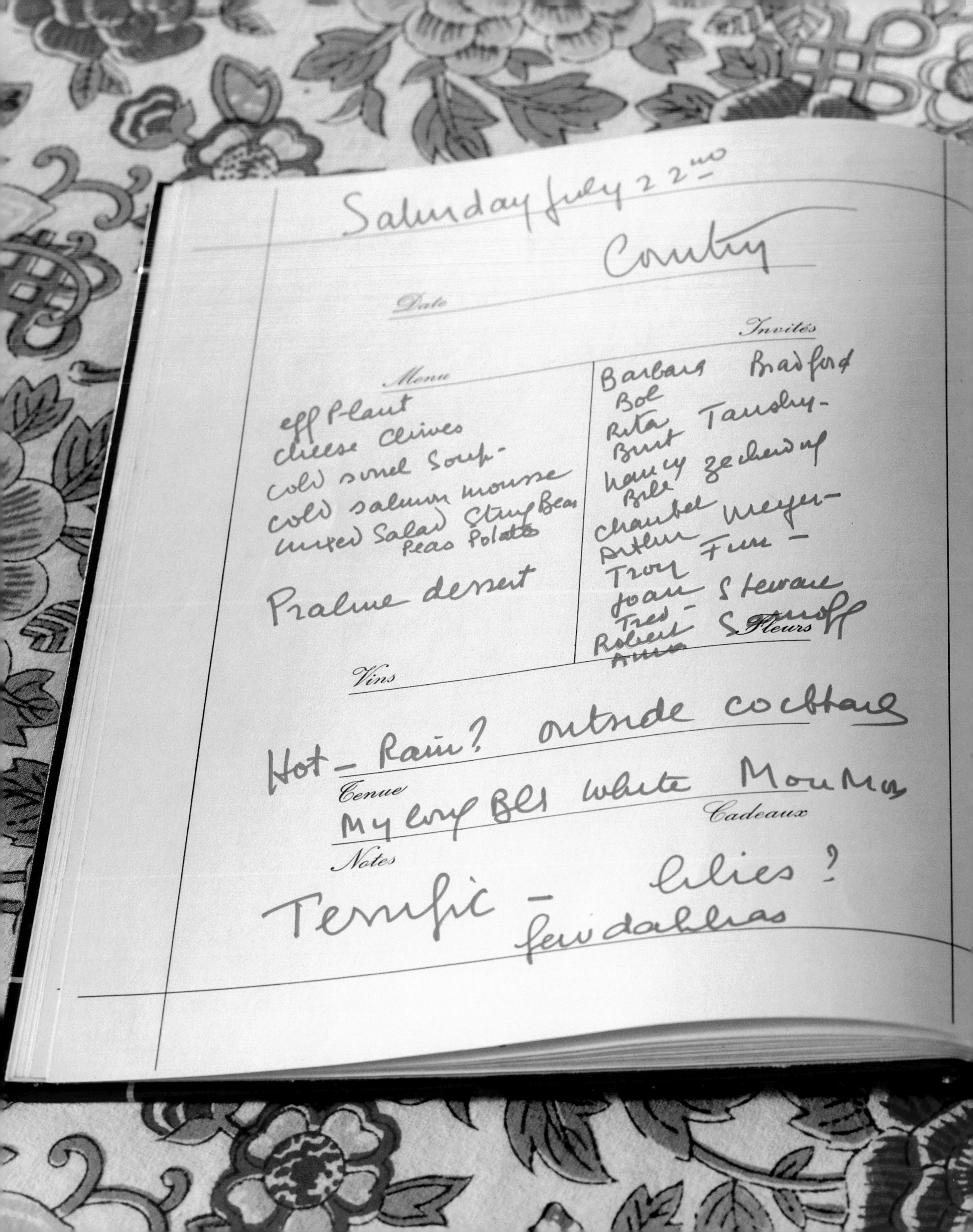

Saturday July 22nd

Date

Country

Invités

Menu

egg Plant
cheese chives
cold sorrel Soup -
cold salmon mousse
mixed Salad string Beans
       Peas Potatos

Praline dessert

Barbara Bradford
Bob
Rita Tanshy -
Burt
Nancy zichendorf
Bill
Chambel Meyer -
Arthur
Troy Finn -
Joan Stewart
Fred -
Robert   Smoff
Anna   *Fleurs*

Vins

Hot - Rain? outside cocktails

Tenue

My long Bea white Moumus

Cadeaux

Notes

Terrific - lilies?
     few dahlias

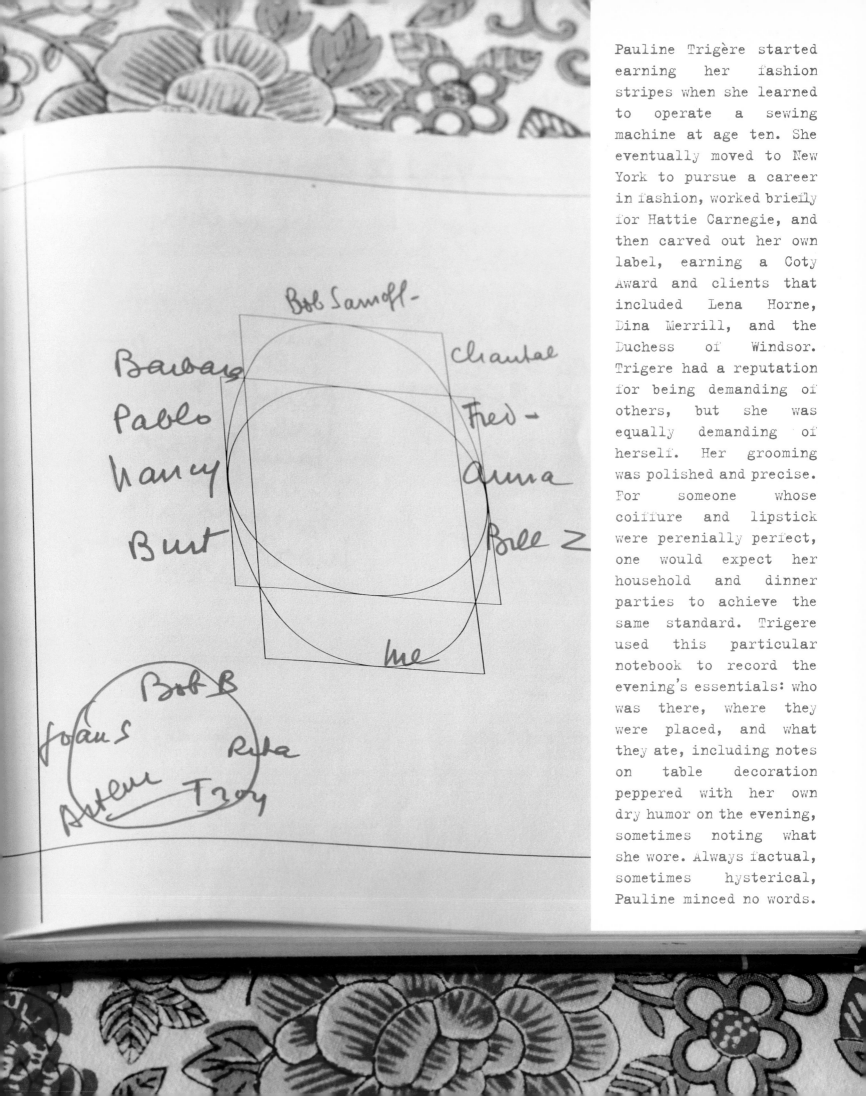

Bob Sarnoff—

Barbara

Pablo

Nancy

Burt

Chantal

Fred—

Anna

Bill Z

me

Bob B

Joans

Rita

Arlene

Troy

Pauline Trigère started earning her fashion stripes when she learned to operate a sewing machine at age ten. She eventually moved to New York to pursue a career in fashion, worked briefly for Hattie Carnegie, and then carved out her own label, earning a Coty Award and clients that included Lena Horne, Dina Merrill, and the Duchess of Windsor. Trigere had a reputation for being demanding of others, but she was equally demanding of herself. Her grooming was polished and precise. For someone whose coiffure and lipstick were perenially perfect, one would expect her household and dinner parties to achieve the same standard. Trigere used this particular notebook to record the evening's essentials: who was there, where they were placed, and what they ate, including notes on table decoration peppered with her own dry humor on the evening, sometimes noting what she wore. Always factual, sometimes hysterical, Pauline minced no words.

PAULINE DE ROTHSCHILD Who else could create clumps of moss punctuated
with grasses and reeds in the center of a dinner table? Pauline de
Rothschild was an original. Her menus and recipes made other women
demented. As Diana Vreeland, her distant cousin, would say, "It will
change the course of history." Pauline appears on countless lists
as a style muse. Few have garnered that reputation consistently and

{ NE PAS OUBLIER }

{ NE PAS OUBLIER }

Charlotte Moss &
The Costume Institute
Invite you to

A conversation on

Pauline de Rothschild

with Mitchell Owens,
New York Design Editor,
Traditional Home Magazine

Home of Charlotte Moss
Street New York City
ember 27, 2006 7:00 pm

with such reverence. Few can claim that they have worked for Hattie Carnegie and Schiaparelli, married a baron, owned residences that have left an indelible mark on design, translated Elizabethan poetry, or were dressed by Balenciaga himself. From financial schizophrenia, luxury, poverty, and back again, Pauline observed life around her, which provided the foundation for a life of intellectual curiosity, the desire for privacy, and a personal aesthetic in which everything was veiled in mesmerizing beauty. Valentine Lawford's account of visiting Pauline at Chateau Mouton is a keen distillation of THE WOMAN, THE LIFE, THE AURA:

To anyone who knew her as Pauline Potter in her New York days, the châtelaine of Mouton seems less to have changed than to have become even more incomparably Pauline. As always, a kind of uniquely personal sunlight streams from her welcome, none the less warm for its suggestions that before one's arrival she had been perfectly happily engaged in secret woods and shadows of her own. Progressively one has noted again the other attributes one remembers--the elegant legs and feet; the silk scarves knotted and reknotted at her neck; the profile, part proud and part vulnerable; the pensive eye that misses nothing; the voice that is both soft and resonant (that wonderful voice that used to be the prerogative of American women brought up in Italy or France); the uncanny ability to dominate a room from a footstool; the yielding sensitivity and thrusting mental keenness; the devastating turn of phrase and the cascades of self-mocking laughter. All are here. Yet all as though only now at long last in their natural element, enclosed in their predestined setting, observed for the first time with perfect clarity; unfolded, enhanced, complete . . . Menus are brought to her in bed. So is a book with photographs of the luncheon and dinner services (one hundred and seventy of them, all told), and other books with swatches of the tablecloths and napkins (an equally prodigious variety) to choose from for the day. Marie, the flower arranger, telephones for instructions before going off on her little motor bicycle in search of moss and branches and blossoms . . . Pauline de Rothschild's views are apt to be as categorical on the meaning of words and phrases as on table settings. The swatch books are full of penciled remarks like mauvais avec les nappes vertes . . . It is a setting that suggests the combined fantasy and neatness of a set of Chinese boxes--in a bed like an arbor sprouting, in a room like an orchard, in a château, in a vineyard, in France. -- Valentine Lawford

Sliced Roasted Filet of Beef
with Argentinean Chimmichurri Sauce
&
Lobster and Crab Jambalaya
with Andouille Sausage
&
Chicken Breast Roulade
stuffed with Dried Cherries and Wild Mushrooms
accompanied by Autumn Fruit Chutney
&
Parsnips Shallots Sweet
Celery Root

"... is as exotic as a unicorn
... subtle as an Egyptian
cat. She is as crisp as
gingham, as sensuous as satin,
and as inscrutable as velvet."
— WYATT COOPER

Sylvia Weinstock is who you go to when you want a cake. It is not really a cake; it is pure magic. The shape, the spun sugar, the fondant she sculpts with the skill of Canova. For this dinner I knew what I wanted: a gingham cake topped with a swan and Gloria's logo surrounded by beautiful flowers associated with her. The tulips represent her iconic fabric for Bloomcraft. I remember the hand-painted glassware she designed with lily of the valley. A cake collage!

I have a scrapbook on Gloria Vanderbilt who attained icon status to me in the early '70s. Gloria was a sensation then because of her designs and her artwork. I followed what she did with gingham fabric, using it generously and luxuriously and making it look rich--more like silk lampas. I admired and aspired to design like she did then, watching her collage, and lacquer floors with patchwork. Gloria had a fearless little-girl quality that made her unconcerned with what others thought. She just did it. She had a style of her own and others followed. So, in my twenties I was encouraged to follow suit as well. I have been collaging ever since. Fast forward to 2010 and the publication of Wendy Goodman's book, GLORIA. Having lunch with Wendy shortly before, I suggested a dinner party at home to celebrate the book. As we discussed various details, I mentioned making a party favor for everyone. Wendy then proceeded to quote Wyatt Cooper: "She is as exotic as a unicorn and as subtle as an Egyptian cat. She is as crisp as gingham, as sensuous as satin, and as inscrutable as velvet." I said, "That's perfect. I leave for a holiday in Egypt next week." To which Wendy replied, ". . . and you will return with fifty statues of cats!" And I did. And found the perfect velvet bag lined in satin for each one.

HOW TO CREATE CHRISTMAS ENCHANTMENT

How to turn out your own romantic wrappings
Ideas from Gloria Vanderbilt

When House & Garden asked Gloria Vanderbilt (Mrs. Wyatt Cooper) if she would some Christmas presents for us, she said she would, and found herself "doing five coll the same time. The top of each box and the four sides." Here are four of her fantas on the next page Mrs. Cooper will tell you what you need and how to proceed to your own romantic wrappings. A painter since she was a child, Mrs. Cooper beca ested in collage a few years ago and has worked on it so hard that she is now, as going right to the top of the tree. In her recently published *Gloria Vanderbilt B lage*, she quotes her dictionary's definition of the technique as "composing a by pasting on a single surface various materials not normally associated with on Her own definition is "a puzzle with a million answers, all correct." She also feel posing a work of art (which she can't help doing) is not nearly so important as the fun in-volved. "Anybody can do it, and you're apt to find the necessary materials right on your own shelves. At this very moment, I'm impatiently waiting for some sheets with blue and red flowers to wear out. The print will be marvelous in a future collage!" *(Continued)*

"In a collage, try always to include something you love."

"Unconsciously, we make collages everyday without knowing it," says Gloria Vanderbilt Cooper. "Whenever a woman gets a certain look in her eye and dashes to a table to rearrange the objects displayed there, it may seem like just puttering to her husband, but she's really making a tabletop collage. That's what collage is—arranging and rearranging as your impulses move you. And although wrapping a present in the manner of a collage is far simpler than doing an actual picture, the basics are the same. So, first of all, gather your materials. I keep an arsenal of supplies in my studio—colored papers, fabrics, old lace, paper lace, ribbons, photographs, greeting cards, valentines, aluminum foil, cutout flowers, what have you. Don't attempt anything until you have a stockpile, and try to build it with things that have a special appeal for you. You'll also need a good pair of scissors, and a white glue. I use *Sprayment*, which works like hair spray.

"Now, since a Christmas present is so very personal, think of the friend you are giving it to before you wrap it. For instance, my oldest and best friend is Carol Matthau, Mrs. Walter Matthau. She's a springtime kind of girl, beautiful, sentimental, mad about flowers. Before I wrapped her present [page 48], I put together a little assembly of things that reminded me of her—apple green tissue, three kinds of flowered ribbon, a braid of embroidered silk roses, a band of Spanish lace, a marvelous old valentine with a little girl in a pink coat and hat edged with ermine, some sprays of paper lilies of the valley, and some funny little Victorian paper Christmas trees. I wrapped the box in tissue, cut the little girl out of the valentine and mounted her on silver lace paper, then experimented with what should go where. Try never to glue anything down until you have an arrangement that really pleases you. Just move things about until something clicks, and *that's it.* When I had Carol's arrangement the way I wanted it, I glued everything down, tied on the ribbons, and added a gold paper medallion with a written greeting to Carol pasted in its center. Remember, someone else might assemble the same elements in quite another way and achieve a totally different effect. That's the wonderful thing about collage. You have no one to please but yourself, and you can do anything at all that gives you the satisfaction of having created something all your own. Don't think about it, just do it.

"Always, I try to include something I am very fond of—a photograph, a bit of embroidery, perhaps a pressed flower. I find that my affection for it influences the form the collage takes, probably because personal feelings, for me, are a much stronger guide than any training in art. For my husband, for example, I wrapped a present in red tissue —he loves red—then framed a favorite photograph of our two little boys and me in a white and silver valentine that I mounted on petals of green and hot pink tissue. As I always do, I cut out bits of pattern in the lace so the colors beneath would glint through, and to let the elements *breathe.* It adds to the delicacy. I tied up the box with a red and white stylized ribbon, cherry red and moss green rope yarn, and a beautiful old black velvet ribbon with purple, orange, and gold flowers. It looked as if it had belonged to the Medicis.

"And now, wrap away. You'll find, as I did, that the more you develop your inner response to things, the more your imagination will grow, and out of this you will arrive at your own personal style."

Charlotte!
still dreaming . . .

of magical evening

gloria vanderbilt

November 11, 2010

Gloria

Charlotte Moss and Barry Friedberg

cordially invite you for dinner

to celebrate

Hutton Wilkinson's new book

More Is More

&

Tuesday, October 27, 2009

at eight o'clock in the evening

at their home

Rsvp to Jean Mc Nally

Attire
Dupioni Inspired

Anyone that knows Hutton Wilkinson knows that *More* is *More* is his motto, possibly even in his nightly prayers—NOT just the title of his book. Who could be more fun to have a party for than Hutton, whose own dinners—and costumes—are legendary. And what a good excuse to have Sylvia Weinstock make one of her amazing cakes a la Dawnridge? No one does it better or more personally, and deliciously.

MORE IS MORE

TONY DUQUETTE

Stealing Magnolias. Deb Shriver is a life force powered by some amazing energy source we all wish we had the formula for. When you are with Deb, you better be alert and on your game because this funny, fast-talking, sharp-as-a-tack, Southern Belle may leave you in the dust. Deb Shriver is a Steel Magnolia of the first order and someone I have admired since the first time we met and "buzzed" about our Southern connections, affections, and predispositions.

Luncheon for
Deb Shriver
&
Stealing Magnolias

Crab Maison

Iceberg Wedge with Smoked Bacon
Buttermilk Dressing

Grits a Ya Ya

Pan Seared Breast of Poussin
Classic Creole Sauce

Corn Pudding

Pimento Lima Beans

Cardamon Scented Whipped Sweet Potatoes

Scalloped Tomatoes

Keith's Pimento Cheese Spread

Hot Crusty Buttermilk Biscuits
Sweet Butter

Banana Trifle
Praline Cake
Coffee, Tea

Creole Kumquat Champagne Cocktail

1994 Château Ducru Beaucaillou Saint Julien

2008 Ladoucette Pouilly-Fumé

December 10, 2010

Holiday Lunch?

You know how hard it can be to schedule a lunch with some of your girlfriends? Weeks can go by with commitments, work, and travel before you can finally sit and have a conversation. So a holiday luncheon is a way to get forty together, so you not only can have face-time with them, but they can all see each other, too. Who really needs an excuse anyway? Not me, it's only lunch.

Holiday Luncheon for the Girls
December 9, 2011

Luter's Virginia Country Ham
with Homemade Spiced Plum-Pear Chutney
Crab Maison

...milk Biscuits with Pimento Cheese

... Sweet Potatoes with Nutmeg
...y Braised Collard Greens
...as and Peas with Fresh Mint
...Grape Tomatoes with Basil

...with Bourbon Whipped Cream
...Pecan Pralines
...Layer Cake

...nay from Vineyard Seven and Eight
2008, Brewer-Clifton Pinot Noir
2007, Schramsberg Blanc de Blanc

Noël

INFINITE VARIETY

Why do some people almost obsessively make scrapbooks? Perhaps to record family history or special events in life, to salvage something from change, or to reflect accomplishment. I read somewhere that "all we can hope for is to be remembered."

In our library, my husband has compiled fifty-four beige linen-covered scrapbooks with dark brown leather labels, dated 1929 to 2010, with titles like "Chicago," "World Trip," "Denmark," "Wedding," "William McC Blair III," "La Fiorentina," "The Philippines," "Washington," "New York." They go beyond family photographs, providing historical perspective with articles on friends, births, deaths, telegrams, speeches, newspaper clippings, social events, Christmas cards with children growing up over the years.

There is another set of twenty-two books that are quite different, which belong to me. Bound in cream parchment with pale green silk, with title like "French," "Italian," "American," or "English Decoration," "Apart from Others," "European Gardens," "Far Away," "Inspired Lives," "Distant Pleasures," "Scattered Flowers." They are a selective and personal choice of pictures ranging from rooms to ruins, individuals to architecture, and deeply admired paintings to beautiful gardens, sculpture, and fragments of lives of interesting individuals who were creative and imaginative.

A wonderful and unconventional friend of mine, Rory Cameron, kept amazing scrapbooks unlike any others I had seen, a record of his most discerning taste. For many summers I visited the Villa Fiorentina, Rory's unforgettable house on Saint-Jean-Cap-Ferrat and had access to these books. They reflected a sense of the past, but the overriding content was a visual journey examining what he loved. Spontaneously, in no orderly fashion, he assembled his own accomplished photos of friends and places, as his world was very much about travel. His insatiable curiosity and remarkable spirit of adventure resulted in his writing books on India, Egypt, Australia, the New World, the eighteenth-century voyages of Captain Cook—the history, the people, the customs, the flowers, the birds, and often including material from travel writers of other periods. What is especially sad is Rory's scrapbooks seem to have disappeared. I have inquired endlessly where they might be. They became the inspiration for mine.

My scrapbooks are quite random and haphazard, as they were not assembled in an orderly or methodical fashion and collated as the years went by. They reflect fifty years of ripping pages from glorious magazines—American, French, Italian and British *Vogue, Connaissance des Arts, L'oeil, Country Life, Paris Match*—and from auction and gallery catalogs. Also, collecting postcards from years of travel, sightseeing, and museum going, plus very unskilled snapshots. Everything was accumulated and crowded into Italian-paper-covered boxes, unsorted, not dated, kept idiosyncratically. Then we moved after thirty-nine years in Washington to New York; it was the moment to approach the disorder and simplify.

My volumes were finally put together by the hugely talented Paul Vogel, whom I met when he repaired some of my treasured books. I had not forgotten once seeing in one of the oldest Venetian paper shops a collection of Latin books

being unimaginably beautifully rebound for the Vatican, and I realized Paul Vogel could create something similarly impeccable. I decided on parchment bindings and end papers from wonderful Venetian hand-printed sheets collected over many years. (He devised a way the books could always be taken apart, which means you can change your mind. We would receive the blank pages then do the layouts and, using double-faced tape, affix the photos and then send back to Mr. Vogel.)

The books predominantly focus on women, as women seem frequently to make a different kind of mark in the world. Think of women of unique intelligence, charm, and imagination: from Liliane de Rothschild, Lulu de Waldner, Jayne Wrightsman, Pauline de Rothschild, Helene Rochas, Louise de Vilmorin, Lesley Blanche, Nancy Lancaster, and Isak Dinesen to Mary Lasker, Amanda Harlech, Oatsie Charles, Marguerite Littman, and Rosine Bemberg. However, perhaps my favorite scrapbooks are called "Infinite Variety." These are mostly what I think of as magical combinations—ranging from photos by Lord Snowdon of ghostly Arabian horses in the fog followed by the Rothko Chapel in Houston to an image of a great black evening dress by John Galliano from the *AngloMania* exhibition in the English period rooms of the Met. (The mannequin is looking out wearing the more than twenty-five pounds of layered taffeta, and there were the sound effects of somewhat agitated birds.) There are Bronzino portraits and Liotard pastels, the Baroda pearls photographed on sand, a Nureyev nude by Richard Avedon, wildflowers by Irving Penn, a fascinating article on the Miao people of China, the Green Vault of Dresden, and the Gates of Paradise—the Ghiberti doors in Florence. Another favorite is a sightseeing book, "Distant Pleasures," which includes the Faisonerie, Schloss Pillnitz, Villa Cornaro, and the Rundale outside Riga.

These books are a collection of very beautiful photographs, compelling to me and atmospheric, mostly all places I have been, only a few unvisited but admired—quite simply, things one must see again, and the memories they evoke. The books are about people I knew of distinctive and memorable taste in the way they lived. They were made in an effort to keep things that are admired less fleeting. They involve life experiences in what might be called a visual memoir.

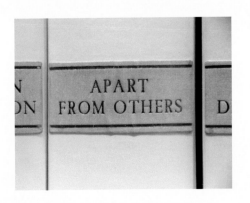

All best
Deeda

A **HOME** IS AN AUTOBIOGRAPHY

Who among us has never been struck, upon entering a room for the first time, by its particular atmosphere, the indefinable perfume given off by it? —*Robert Polidori* You do not say the same thing in one room as you say in another, that's how sensitive a room is. —*Louis Kahn* Growing up, I absorbed the Southern obsession with place, and place can seem to me somehow an extension of the self. —*Frances Mayes* Houses of the best taste are like clothes of the best tailors—it takes their age to show us how good they are. —*Henry James* Stay at home and don't wear out your shoes. —*Yiddish Proverb* The charm, the attraction, character, what you will, of the house is that it has grown over the years in a haphazard sort of way . . . It is a conglomeration of style and periods of furniture and decoration . . . There is no theme, no connecting style. Each room is a jumble of old and new. —*The Duchess of Devonshire* We said there wasn't no home like a raft, after all. Other places do seem so cramped up and smothering, but a raft don't. You feel mighty free and easy and comfortable on a raft. —*Mark Twain* A room in which we surround ourselves with the things we love not only makes us comfortable but also becomes a means of expressing ourselves of establishing our personal sense of style. —*Lisa Newson* I'd rather be shut up in a very modest cottage, with my books, my family and a few old friends, dining on simple bacon, and letting the world roll on as it liked, than to occupy the most splendid post which any human power can give. —*Thomas Jefferson* Home was quite a place when people stayed there. —*E. B. White*

ALBUM 1

Living rooms
Entertainment rooms
Reception rooms

Tall, regal, intelligent, and mysterious Evangeline Bruce was one of America's greatest "ambassadresses." As an author, a diplomat's daughter, and the wife of a diplomat as well, she combined the best of what she inherited to make a life filled with graciousness, efficiency, and beauty. As author of *Napoleon and Josephine: An Improbable Marriage*, she found the year 1795 in Paris to be ". . . the most exciting year in history. . . ." as Paris was jubilant over the end of the terror. Evangeline and David Bruce began their married life in Paris in 1947 in an apartment that would link them to the revolution, in an ironic way. They lived on the rue de Lille in the apartment that belonged to the Princess de Lamballe, loyal friend of Marie Antoinette. Poignantly, Evangeline Bruce died on the two hundredth anniversary of that "most exciting year."

I have two scrapbooks in my collection owned and composed by Evangeline Bruce. These books came to me from the antiquarian bookdealer, Kinsey Marable. The books were prepared in a casual manner and include photos of rooms she liked: black-and-white snapshots of her own homes and those of others. On each page, styles repeat themselves over and over again--a testimony to the clearly established point of view and personal style of their creator.

AN ENGLISH DREAM

BY VALENTINE LAWFORD

Anyone quite so authentically English and authentically American could only be a Virginian.

I first met Mrs. Nancy Lancaster in war-time Britain. She may not welcome the reminder. Even implied compliments make her wince. But I remember how she sold her American family's loved estate of Mirador at considerable personal loss when England was more than usually in need of dollars, and how she chose to become a British subject when the war was at its height. I remember too how, married then to Ronald Tree, the Parliamentary Private Secretary to the Minister of Information, she and he were for weekend after weekend tireless hosts to Winston Churchill and his retinue at Ditchley Park, one of the loveliest country houses in England. As Churchill has gratefully recorded, it was considered safer than his official country house of Chequers, particularly on nights of a full moon. What he has not recorded is that it was also incomparably more attractive and comfortable.

But I remember best how I would sigh with relief to find that occasionally she had been invited to the same weekday, war-time, "austerity" London luncheon as I had. For she was that rewarding phenomenon, a woman as handsome as she was humorous, and all the more impressive because what she most lacked was self-importance—unless it were a

Above and opposite: These very exuberant chairs, Chinese in the gothic taste, were once owned by Nancy Lancaster. The photo resides in Evangeline Bruce's scrapbook, as she, coincidentally, was the chairs' next owner. Years later, I received a call from Gerald Bland and Kinsey Marable. They said in unison, "Charlotte, we have a pair of chairs that you should own." And, here they are . . . Who could say NO?

The double salon; the dividing wall, a fireplace facing two ways.
White walls countered with flowers—real and woven.
The old mill beams countered with parlour furniture.

Dior

DECORATION

satin
...talli, three
...ir are cov-
call *tilleul*.
an alcove
baldaquin
alcove holds
tique needle
doré. The
Grandpierre

DETAILS
FROM THE
PARIS HOUSE
OF THE DUKE AND
DUCHESS OF WINDSOR

The Duchess of Windsor prefers to entertain ten,
although her table seats sixteen. "We consider
dinner for sixteen practically a court ball," she

FLAIR

A library is painted on the pipe organ

Elsie any exercises

The watercolors of Elsie de Wolfe's bedroom at Trianon and her Treillage
music room had been known to me for some time prior to the Christie's
auction a number of years ago. Both works were painted by William Ellis
Ranken, coincidentally, the same artist of the first interior purchased
for my collection--that of Joseph Duveen's drawing room. Elsie and Duveen
knew each other well, as they collaborated on the decoration of the home
owned by Henry Clay Frick, now the Frick Collection.

I could not think of anything more personal, so
totally Elsie, than her personal photo album: photos
of Elsie pasted into a book by her hand, a book
containing her favorite photos of herself. And to
be clear about it, on the cover she scrawled "Me"
with a pen. There you have it.

ME

I am going to make everything around me beautiful, that will be my life. Never complain, never explain. Today is the tomorrow you worried about yesterday. A house will speak for a woman's life... it is a dead giveaway. I have never heard of anyone who had beauty around him murdering anybody or making someone else unhappy. From the moment I was conscious of ugliness and its relation to myself and my surroundings, my one preoccupation was to find my way out of it. Plenty of optimism and white paint. There are no pockets in a shroud. You search the world for beauty, for beautiful things to live with... and then... in comes your husband wearing some awful old trenchcoat... and ruins the effect. A house should be a synthesis of comfort, practicality, and tradition. I was born with the courage to live. Only those are unwise who have never dared to be fools. What is the goal? A house that is like the life that goes with it, a house that gives us beauty as we understand it—and beauty of a nobler kind that we may grow to understand. In my escape, I came to the meaning of beauty. —*Elsie de Wolfe*

Hotel Plaza

Elsie → + the acrobat 1929

de Gonorofe

Elsie

ELSIE DE WOLFE.

Muchette

Elsie + her Locomobile
New York

ASPEN

ROUND TRAY. Loochoo red lacquer. 112.

Rooms reflect who you are, your choice of objects, how you arrange them, and the color
of the backdrop you select to frame it all. The rooms featured in the following pages
from my homes in Aspen, New York, and East Hampton represent the three-dimensional
life of color collages that started the design conversation for each space.
While these collages organize color thoughts, others might define the furnishings
and the feeling one is after. This lacquer-red collage, for example, illustrates
the inspirations behind the living room in my Aspen home (PRECEDING PAGE, RIGHT).

Like looking through a viewfinder, scrutinizing the most minute detail, in private and in darkness: a house is an autobiography. How could it not be? Every object, the color on the wall, the selection and arrangement of furniture, the books, the flowers, the fragrance, the housekeeping . . . the ambiance. Every last detail spells you.

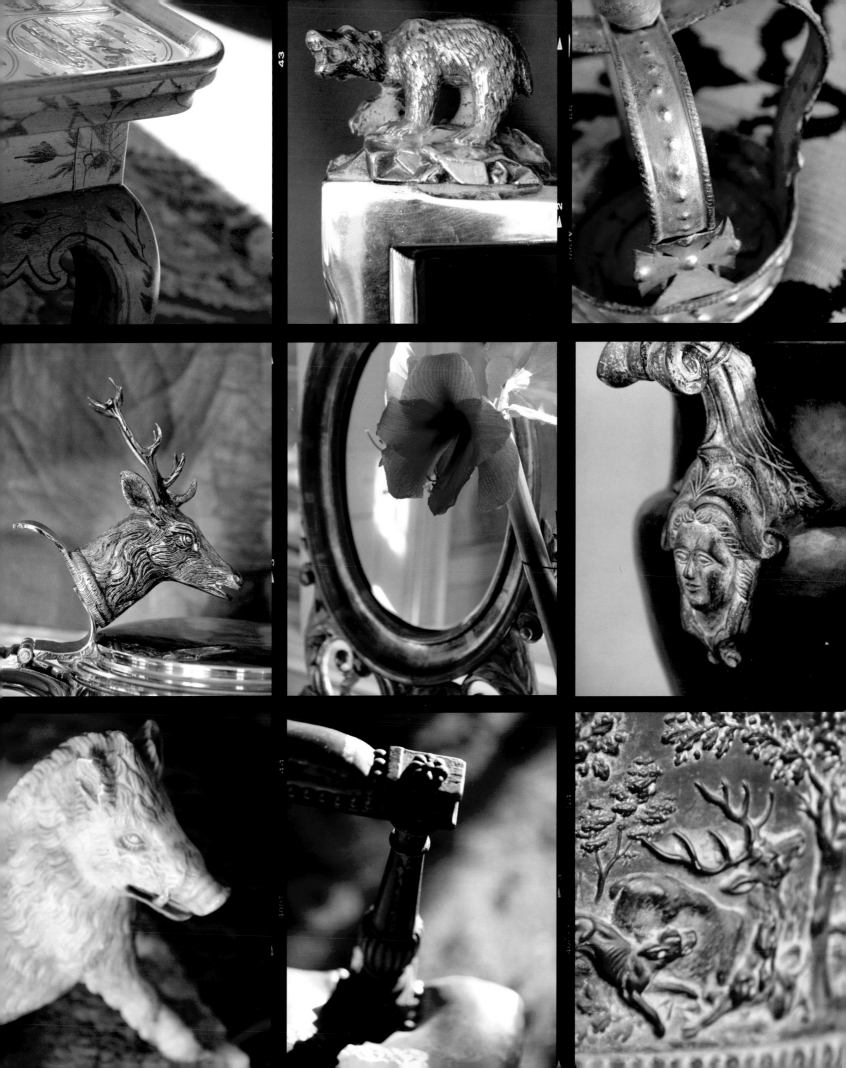

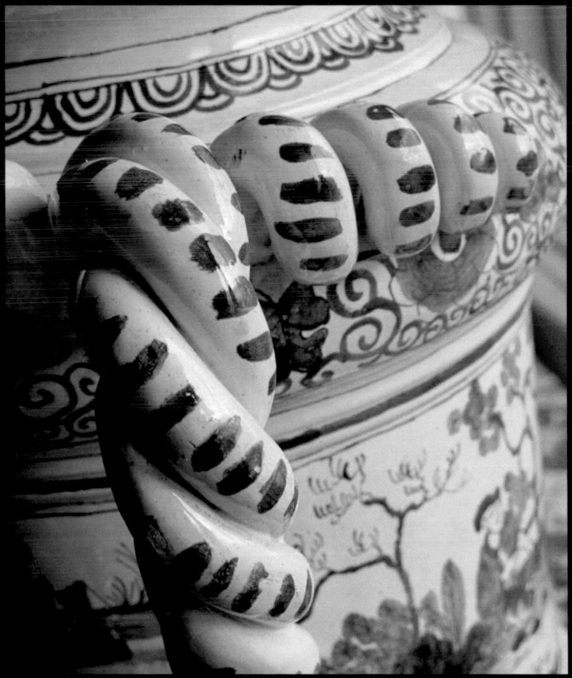

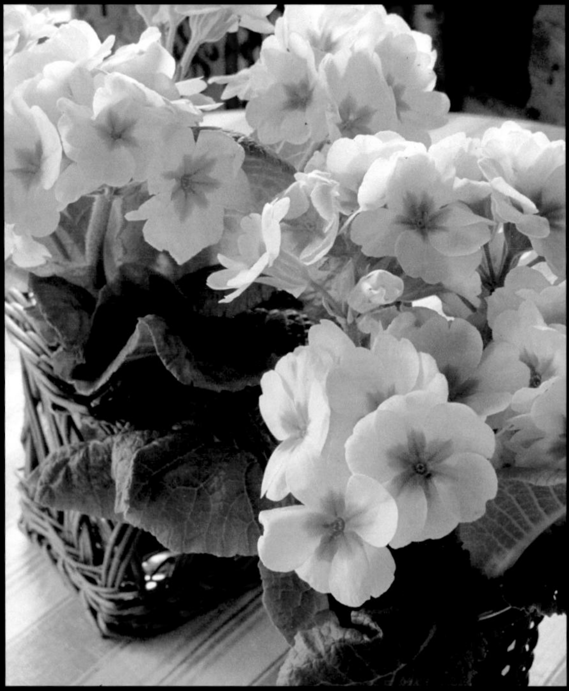

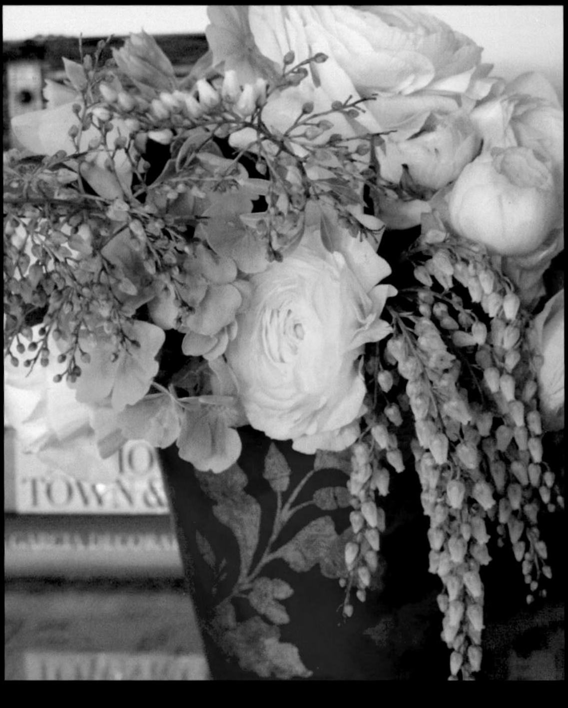
TOWN &

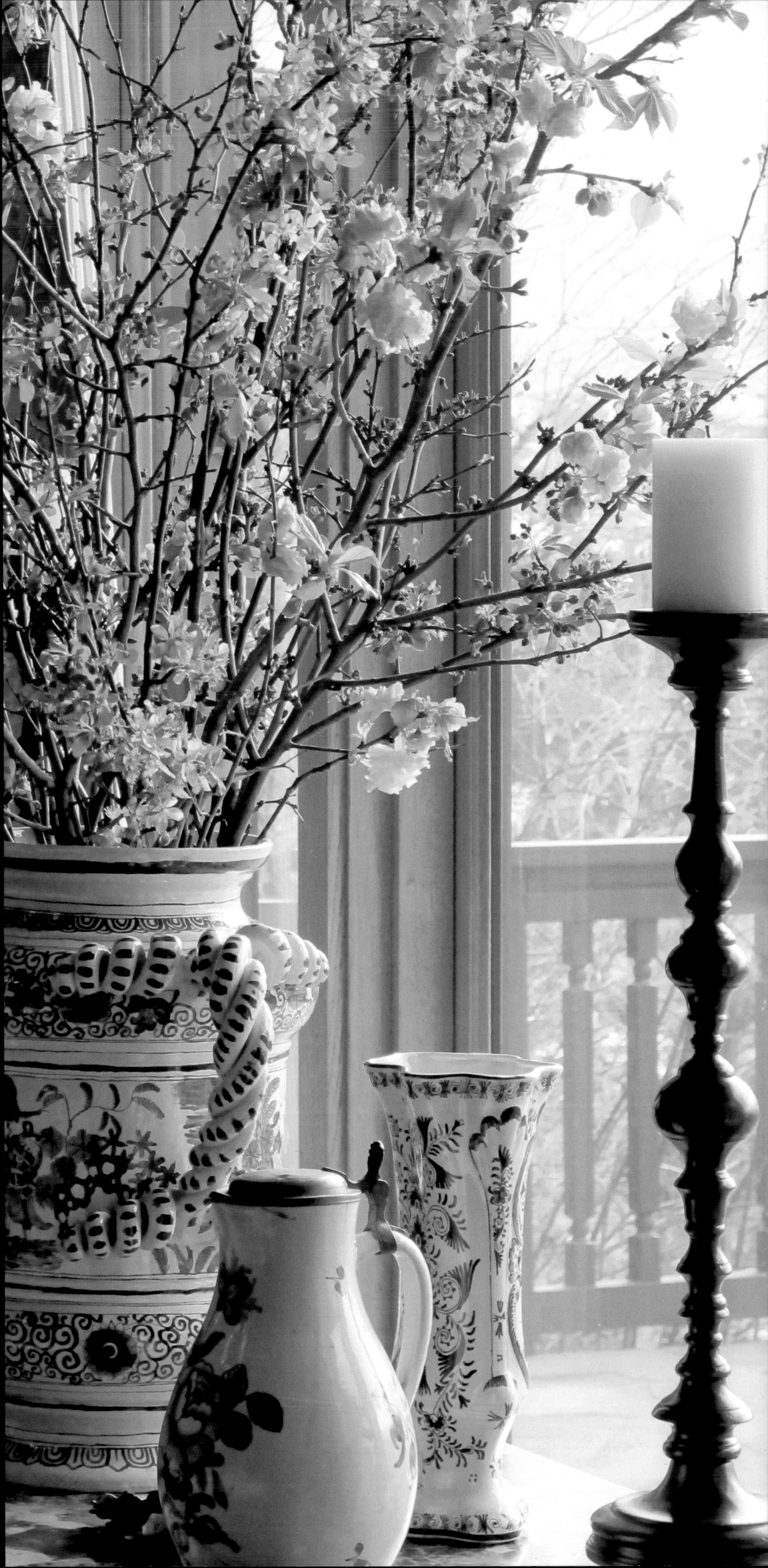

NEW YORK

A collection that just "happened": drawings, engravings, gouache, and pencil sketches of women. Years of decorating and shopping have produced items too numerous to count. They come and they go, but most remain constant companions, like this wall of women who all seem to have one trait in common--attitude.

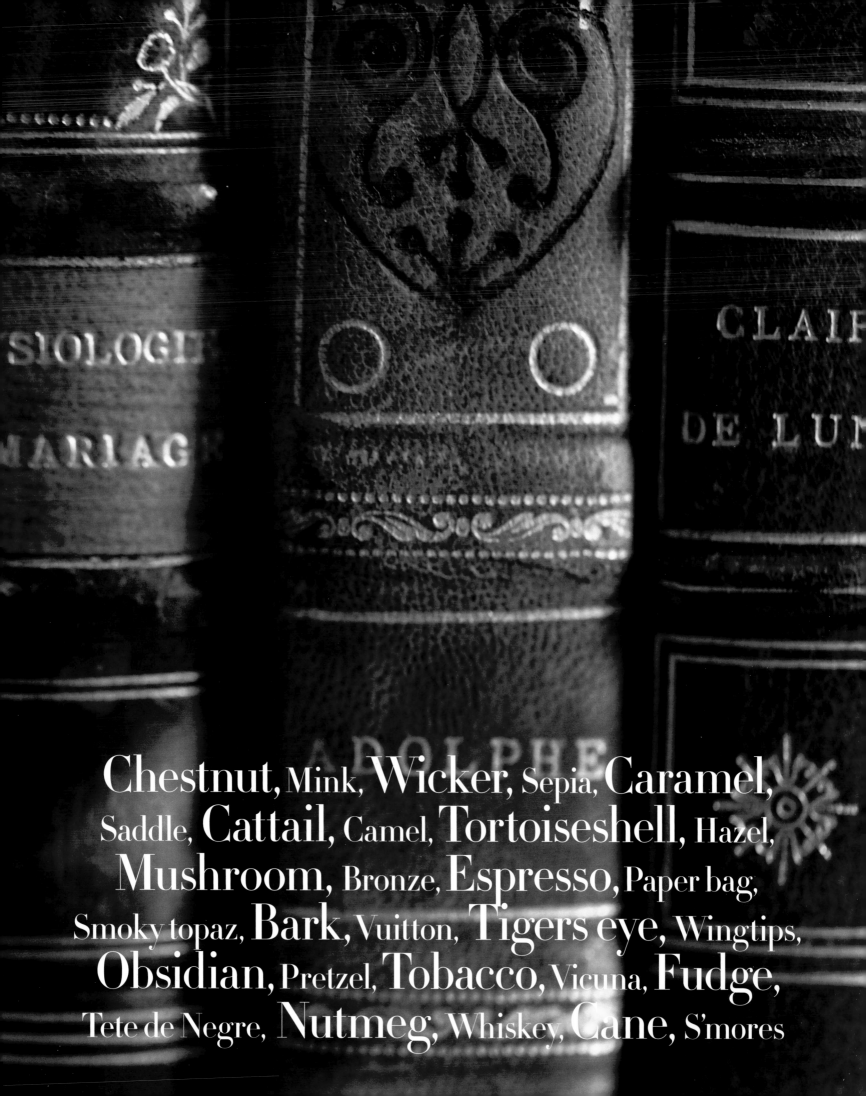

Chestnut, Mink, Wicker, Sepia, Caramel, Saddle, Cattail, Camel, Tortoiseshell, Hazel, Mushroom, Bronze, Espresso, Paper bag, Smoky topaz, Bark, Vuitton, Tigers eye, Wingtips, Obsidian, Pretzel, Tobacco, Vicuna, Fudge, Tete de Negre, Nutmeg, Whiskey, Cane, S'mores

EMBROIDERY INSPIRATION
Penn and Fletcher in New York can interpret just about anything in embroidery. Thumbing through a neo-classical patterns book, I selected an interlocking pattern for the headboard and footboard of my bed. After making thread color selections, we worked out the scale and the location.

For years I have worked with color day in and day out, but when it came to creating my bathroom and dressing room I knew exactly what I wanted--white. "Plenty of optimism and white paint," Elsie de Wolfe said. Well, I have the white paint, and each day I start there and pray I do it optimistically.

Violet . . . orchid . . . amethyst . . . lavender . . . All variations on a theme, but try using just words . . . Sometimes words fail . . . A picture can be a defining moment.

EAST
HAMPTON

The living room in East Hampton is in part a library. Three walls of books, a double-height ceiling, plenty of seating for reading, this room is the center of the house. I often work at a table here because I can see the garden, hear the birds, and be close to my books.

ABOVE: This table is a wonderful example of a type of collage that became a fashionable art form in the eighteenth century: *arte povera*. In Europe, but particularly in Venice, where it was a professional occupation, *arte povera* was popular with artists and dilettantes alike. Printers such as Remondini near Bassano created figures and motifs to be cut out, hand-painted, then lacquered onto pieces of furniture, just like this one.

A year-round sleeping porch and studio, this is my space. A desk for writing,
an architect's desk for my collage work, a large bookcase for all the essential
elements, images, and materials for collage. An antique daybed for a nap, a
relaxed place to read, or the perch for Oscar and Daisy while I work.

PUTTERING: IT JUST IS

Today I spent the day puttering around the house reacquainting myself with my own home, moving slowly from room to room, looking, assessing, editing.

Over the years, I have redecorated (what do you expect?), tweaked, and refreshed. Recently, I re-wallpapered the dining room and added new curtains. Beige. It was a revelation--self-revelation, that is. I like the soothing, calming shades of beige. Now, the ripple effect is this: a new color can create chaos. It causes you to reevaluate the other rooms. Don't start!! Forget thinking about the decorating. Now back to puttering.

Moving onto the flower room, I organize my gardening articles, gardens to visit, notes, and files--what's working, my plant "wish list," etc. This is my Zen.

The great thing about puttering: it has no goal. Such a relief. It just IS.

MY VISUAL INSTRUCTION

Scrapbooks have been in my life forever. They are visible manifestations of my parents' desire to create memories, order them, and bind them into actual decorative objects—objects by which they desired to be surrounded. So scrapbooks to me have always seemed the most perfectly normal things to have—long before I realized my parents were obsessive-compulsive about photography (my father), with a terrifying instinct toward hoarding rolls and rolls of film like a mad archivist (my mother). Along with obelisks and urns and *tempiettos*, I understood scrapbooks to be artifacts that one just *had*. Now I see that I have been spoiled rotten by our scrapbooks and the record they have kept.

Our family scrapbooks have structured my memories, generally, and many of my notions of art and architecture, specifically. When I look through our family scrapbooks, of which there are dozens, I learn and relearn the sequence of my parents' lives together: their marriage, the entrance into the world of my sister and me, our youth, and times when we did various things as a family. In this way, they seem to me like reverse Russian stacking dolls—they are small objects that reveal big ideas. On the one hand, they are just books; on the other, they contain visions of rooms, houses, buildings, and images of grand family events. My parents always stressed that if our apartment caught fire, we would have to jump out the window with our scrapbooks. This sounds creepy, but we lived on the second floor. (Actually: still creepy!)

As a designer who is the daughter of a designer, my tutelage in design began very young. My father was not shy about proselytizing. He lectured whenever he had a chance—and sometimes when he didn't. Only later did I realize that my visual instruction began long before his verbal onslaught. My training began when looking through the scrapbooks. I literally was able to see the way my father saw things, because he, as the photographer, was setting up the shots (a metaphor for his being the boss, which he would have relished). In this way, I have seen the façade of buildings captured just so. I have pored over tablescapes that were perfectly orchestrated. I have seen enfilades captured in just the way he liked to view them. Looking in a visual person's scrapbook is a little like entering a cult. It is like what Flaubert once said: the role of the author is to be "present everywhere and visible nowhere." Twelve years after my father's

death, my parents' scrapbooks—their ways of seeing things—had a huge and visible influence upon the look of the first book I published.

In my senior year at Brown University, I took a wonderful seminar called "Autobiography." We read a wide range of autobiographies from Rousseau and Bertrand Russell to Oscar Wilde and Lillian Hellman. We spent much of the class extrapolating meaning from what the authors had chosen to write or not write about themselves, regardless of whether or not it was actually true. To my mind, assembling the content for a scrapbook is like writing an autobiography—choosing highlights to include and editing out the unseemly. It is doubly so for a person who has a passion for the visual arts. So in my scrapbooks, I have great images of the Florence Duomo or of Oranienbaum outside of St. Petersburg or of Drottningholm near Stockholm—and no pictures of me eating or of my husband's bald spot or of feet.

When I graduated from college, right before resuming my job at my father's office and before graduate school, my father offered me the opportunity to accompany my mother and him on a trip to Florence and Venice with the trustees of the American Academy of Rome. At the last minute, a work commitment kept my father at home, and my mother and I were left to go to Italy without him (watch out, shoe stores!). This was one of the most magical trips of my life. Michael Graves was one of our cohorts on this trip, and one day I found myself chatting with him outside a beautiful house in Fiesole. Suddenly he said, "Alexa, can you tell me what is wrong with the façade we are looking at?" Let me say that nothing could be more terrifying to a twenty-one-year-old interested in design than being asked an architectural question by Michael Graves without forewarning. Nothing. Looking at the building and reviewing what I had seen of buildings in my life and the millions of images I had only seen in my parents' books, I ventured a guess: "It has an even number of windows?" He smiled and nodded, and I made sure never to stand anywhere near him again.

When it comes to scrapbooks, the icing on the cake is that they are beautiful books. I spend a lot of my time ordering library bookcases for my design projects and for myself. Again, there is a lot of selective autobiography to one's bookshelf display. I have my great historical biographies on exhibit, cheek by jowl next to artists' monographs and catalogues raisonnes. (Missing are the romance novels I read with Fabio on the cover and books on eating right for my blood type.) So nothing could be more perfect and personal then a series of scrapbooks. For my parents, they always bound theirs in a bright cherry red leather with "Hampton" embossed on the spine. Mine are a caramel brown with solitary gold Roman numerals (you try putting "Hampton-Papageorgiou" on the side of a book).

While scrapbooking feels as though it could be going by the wayside, there is a large group of people keeping it alive in a new format: bloggers. Just like the office scrapbooks my father began by tearing pages out of *House & Garden* in the 1960s, modern-day bloggers have become our design scrapbookers. If I want to find Billy Baldwin's peacock-blue room with the zigzag painted floor, I Google it, and there it is. I miss the physical experience of a book, but I am grateful for the resource.

Alexa Hampton

LITTLE
PLEASURES

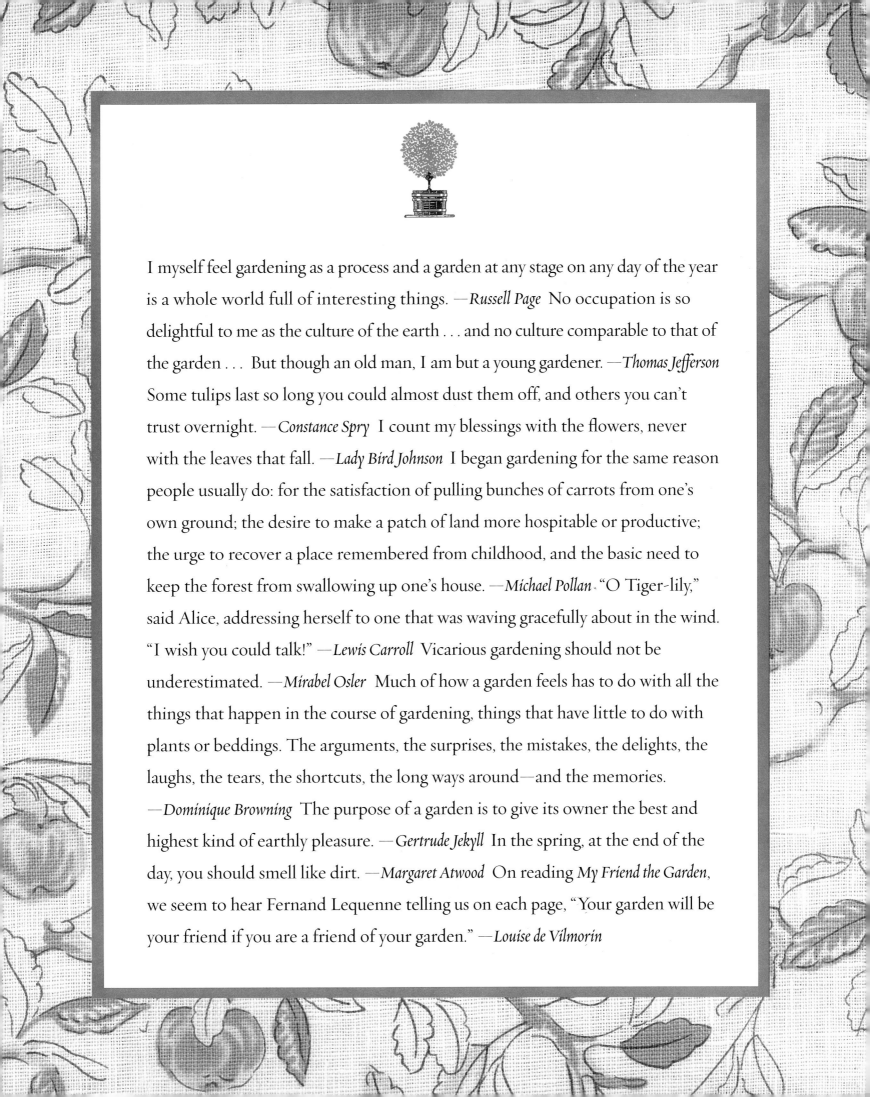

I myself feel gardening as a process and a garden at any stage on any day of the year is a whole world full of interesting things. —*Russell Page* No occupation is so delightful to me as the culture of the earth . . . and no culture comparable to that of the garden . . . But though an old man, I am but a young gardener. —*Thomas Jefferson* Some tulips last so long you could almost dust them off, and others you can't trust overnight. —*Constance Spry* I count my blessings with the flowers, never with the leaves that fall. —*Lady Bird Johnson* I began gardening for the same reason people usually do: for the satisfaction of pulling bunches of carrots from one's own ground; the desire to make a patch of land more hospitable or productive; the urge to recover a place remembered from childhood, and the basic need to keep the forest from swallowing up one's house. —*Michael Pollan* "O Tiger-lily," said Alice, addressing herself to one that was waving gracefully about in the wind. "I wish you could talk!" —*Lewis Carroll* Vicarious gardening should not be underestimated. —*Mirabel Osler* Much of how a garden feels has to do with all the things that happen in the course of gardening, things that have little to do with plants or beddings. The arguments, the surprises, the mistakes, the delights, the laughs, the tears, the shortcuts, the long ways around—and the memories. —*Dominique Browning* The purpose of a garden is to give its owner the best and highest kind of earthly pleasure. —*Gertrude Jekyll* In the spring, at the end of the day, you should smell like dirt. —*Margaret Atwood* On reading *My Friend the Garden*, we seem to hear Fernand Lequenne telling us on each page, "Your garden will be your friend if you are a friend of your garden." —*Louise de Vilmorin*

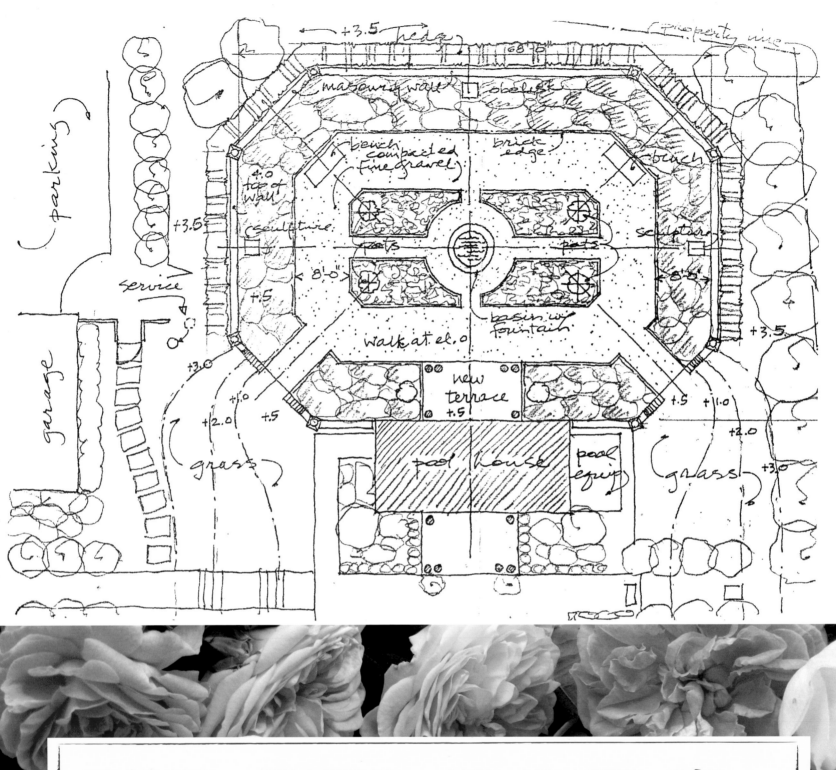

PLOTTED, PLANNED, AND PRAYED FOR

My garden of twenty-plus years: plotted, planned, bulldozed, ripped apart, replanted, prayed for, but--most of all--enjoyed. My scrapbooks remind me time and time again that gardens are living, breathing things; constantly changing, they are "works in progress," and that is all they will ever be, now and forever, amen. The puttering, the planning, the planting, the arranging, that soothing cup of tea, the fragrant pesto for dinner and the salad, the flower arrangements for the table: these are life's little pleasures.

GARDENING FRIENDS

Most gardeners can list for you their blissful moments, and everyone of course has their own definition. I can say without equivocation that the time spent in my potting room is at the top of my list. There are moments of solitude--quietly arranging flowers, trimming a topiary, repotting a creeping fig, taking notes, or referring to some books on herbs.

Then, there are other moments at the end of a long week when I am happy to make flower arrangements for the entire house with music turned up and a glass of wine at hand. Humming quietly, I am "in my element," as my husband says, and everyone knows not to disturb me. After all, I joke with him, "No one can bother you while you are putting on the ninth hole." Indeed, a potting room, shed, or pavilion to a gardener is all the same--a place of our own to do what we love, and where making a mess is, well, just part of the deal. It is the one place in the house where the mess just does not matter.

When you are organized, as in anything, you function happily and productively. Just like a well-organized desk or closet, everything has its place. Among my favorites are a khaki apron and a selection of rubber boots (I love my Missoni boots from Target and my new Hunter florals, a gift from a friend). There are always several hats close by--the favorites--and numerous baskets to choose from for gathering flowers. The one I found in an antique shop in Napa Valley I always grab first. Why? Not because it functions any better . . . but because it is the most beautiful.

OPPOSITE: Watercolor vignettes of my East Hampton garden, given to me as gifts by Gary Bohan, our house manager. I love his soft palette and style, as it evokes more than what the landscape offers.

BOXWO
TERRA

CHOIR DE VERDURE

Early Saturday and Sunday as I gather my dogs, a basket, and camera and go out to the garden, I am always greeted by a chorus of robins: one taking food to a nest hidden in the vines above the arched kitchen garden gate, another near my hammock, and others hidden in a hornbeam hedge.

Bossy crows screech orders to one of the uninvited woodpeckers busy at work on a "project" on one of my oak trees. A red-winged blackbird makes an appearance and the occasional cardinal stands out against the white blossoms of the climbing hydrangea.

Every weekend, same morning welcome, same entertainment. We all go about our business aware of each other's presence but oblivious to others' agendas.

WHATEVER YOU HAVE
IS WHAT YOU'VE GOT

The end of summer announces itself quietly and reluctantly. Roses are on the wane. There is laziness in the herbaceous border, a potager less than plentiful. But clematis paniculata is blanketing anything and everything. The apples will soon be ready for picking, and the figs are producing their second go-round.

   Each year, the last week of August and the first of September, I gather what is still blooming, mixed with leaves, herbs, and often times weeds or wild flowers to create my last bouquet of the summer. I photograph each one as a reminder that whatever you have is what you've got, and with it you can create something beautiful. If it is the last bloom standing, it will be your send-off until the garden ignites next year. The anticipation will kill you.

CHÂTEAU DE GOURDON

At the end of a long, winding road, a former mule path called "Way of the Paradise," Château de Gourdon sits on a rocky promontory overlooking the Valley of the Wolf. Once you see it, you are drawn to it, and even if you were not planning to visit . . . you will. The vision is a siren call. Dating to the twelfth century and built in stages over subsequent centuries, the gardens were my mission. Italian stone lions stand guard on the "Terrace of Honor" where boxwood hedges are trimmed in various ways and look down on the Italian terrace and the rest of the valley. The apothecary garden, an intimate enclosure, is dominated by an unusual oblique sundial. Gourdon is where time stands still.

CHÂTEAU D'AINAY LE VIEIL

The best parts of the gardens here are found within an enclosure. The Verge Sculpte employs the techniques of *La Quintinie* at the potager at Versailles. Espalier of all shapes—apples, pears, figs decorate and delight at every turn. A *parterre de broderie* finished with a tablature in pale blue pays homage to *Le Notre* while a meditation and herbal garden overflows with inspiration for days of gardening.

GARDENS OF EYRIGNAC

The Gardens at Eyrignac were conceived in the 1960s by Gilles Sermadiras, the father of the current owner Patrick Sermadiras. For five hundred years and twenty-two generations, the family has resided at Eyrignac and, together, designs and tends its gardens today. The property is pristine with great care given to every vista: the topiary, clipped and shaped hedges, pyramid-shaped yews, white garden, potager, and a topiary nursery. How the gardens emanate from the manor house struck me immediately as I came into the courtyard. I imagine that a different visual feast awaits at every window.

CHÂTEAU DE HAUTEFORT

For anyone visiting the Aquitaine region in southwestern France, Hautefort is a required visit. One of the most imposing structures of the Perigord region, Hautefort is a château built by two architects, neither of whom were from the region (hence, its unique silhouette). Today, its perfectly maintained French gardens and English park are any gardener's great reward. But Hautefort, as a château, is a feast for the eyes as the decorative arts represented here--from the entry through the apartments-- speak to the scholarship and brilliant management of its foundation.

The furnishings of de Hautefort speak to the generations of families who have inhabited it, loved it, and restored it, and restored it again. A unique and imposing castle rising from a hill in the Perigord overlooking the Bauze and Lourde valleys, Château de Hautefort exudes a warmth, charm, and intellect, echoing its royal origins and the curatorial eyes of subsequent families. Brussels and Aubusson tapestries, seventeenth-and-eighteenth-century Italian busts and urns attributed to Bouchardon, and Louis XVI furniture by Dupain together cultivate the elegant ambience that draws crowds to this tranquil fortress.

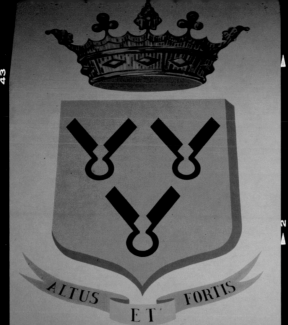

ALTUS ET FORTIS

CHARLES DE NONJON.

LE VIEUX LOGIS

Tucked away in the village of Tremolat, Le Vieux Logis is the only Relais Chateaux in this area of the Perigord. Every morning of my visit here, I awoke to the music of morning doves as the sun was just beginning to illuminate the tips of yew obelisks in the garden. With only twenty-five rooms, some in the main house and some opening directly to gardens, the feeling of privacy equaled that of a large country house. All meals were al fresco with crisp white linens under the fragrant umbrella-like Tilleul, lime blossom trees. A small swimming pool, an oasis on non-garden visitation days, sat in a garden dotted with perfectly clipped round boxwood balls. I chatted with the gardeners and photographed them as they clipped the box shrubs by hand with their rudimentary wooden frames, the same wooden frames that have been used for centuries.

Gardens and pleasure seem inextricably entwined, tied together as in a lovers' knot. Something other than pride or duty keeps us plodding up and down the lawn on a hot afternoon . . . Where do the hazy fantasies—that perhaps imagine the dance of the seven veils on a suburban terrace—come from?
—*Jane Brown*

CHATEAU ET JARDINS DE LOSSE Dwarf boxwood
borders in a Greek key pattern line a path in a walled enclosure. Elsewhere,
the boxwood is rounded and clipped to appear interwoven as if to remind
visitors (in case they could possibly forget) that this is an art form the
French perfected. Nobody does it better, so to speak. In another garden tall
walls of hornbeam create rooms concealing surprises for garden guests.
  As I was leaving, two things caught my eye: a new, very chic hedge of young
hornbeam espalier anchored with a double-step hedge; and a young man trimming
a box hedge--by hand, of course.

MARQUEYSSAC

Boxwood is the dominant theme in the garden at Marqueyssac. In fact, 150,000 plants make up this garden in the Dordogne dating from the seventeenth century. Twice a year, all 150,000 are trimmed by hand.

A long meandering walk some 2,600 feet long takes you to a Belvedere with a panoramic view of the Perigord region. With the hum of cicadas in the background, you can rest and enjoy the view--before you double back along another path. Boxwood clouds are everywhere as you take your garden exploration. A larger garden described as BOXWOOD CHAOS with shrubs resembling boxes tumbling down a hill are just some of the forms adjacent to the château. A nature pavilion houses dioramas of wild fauna from the region, while an aviary of white fantailed pigeons and a sashaying peacock are among the other key elements of château life present there.

CHÂTEAU DE TALCY

Originally established in the thirteenth century, Talcy functioned as a farm estate from the eighteenth century onwards. The restoration of the gardens in 1996 included orchards of espaliered apples and pears. Flower borders were simple, containing few plants and were successful exercises in the effectiveness of repetition and abundance. On the day I visited, there was an exhibition of antique birdcages in the garden, outdoor passages, and throughout the rooms of the château. The styling, the still lifes, the careful selections. Each room was a lesson in decoration: textiles, finishes, furnishings all suited to the ease of country life and infused with the pervasive need for beauty.

Cerisier
Big géant

Scrapbooking in the Digital Age

When I was younger, every time I came across an old scrapbook or photo album in a junk shop or at the flea market, I would feel compelled to rescue it. At home, I'd stare at the young girls in their bathing costumes at the beach in the '20s, or the boys heading off to war posing in front of white clapboard houses with tidy front gardens, and especially at the young couples, often blurry, full of promise and optimism, kissing or ice-skating or sitting on a porch swing. I would wonder about their lives, whether their children cared for them and whether they continued to care for one another. I'd also wonder about the journey of the book itself. These books were true *memento mori*, adrift in the world—containing memories lost without a mind to hold them. Someone had once closely guarded their contents, neatly pasting down images or photo corners onto the pages and carefully writing out captions, before they had ended up forgotten and in my stranger's hands.

I first fell in love with gardens through books: Russell Page's words, Geoffrey Jellicoe's designs, Edith Wharton's travels, Beatrix Farrand's plantings, David Hicks's bossy sense of what was good. When I eventually ventured out to meet these gardens firsthand, those old scrapbooks were my inspiration. With a discontinued-model black-and-white Polaroid Land camera and some other archaic contraption that required turning the backseat of the car into a makeshift film-developing lab, I traced the journey Wharton recorded in her 1904 book *Italian Villas and Their Gardens*. At home, I neatly pasted down photo corners and carefully wrote out captions for each villa: D'Este, Lante, Medici, Torrigiani, and others, including my favorite, the serene and theatrical Villa Gamberaia. Over the years I would do this for other horticultural jaunts and side trips, allowing me to remember not just the gardens but also my feelings about each one. Later when I had become a gardener myself, and then a garden writer, all the ideas and inspiration I stole from each garden I visited ended up as photos and sketches and text all gloriously jumbled on the pages of bursting scrapbooks, still fashioned after those old-fashioned ones from the flea market.

It would seem that scrapbooks would be a relic today. There are, after all, applications for saving imagery culled from anywhere into virtual, shareable, and even shoppable scrapbooks, and digital programs for creating instantly publishable, dust-jacketed hardcover books for your photos. Why bother with an analog album?

Imagine, though, a scene from twenty years from now, where a child finds, say, her grandmother's Pinterest file (the now-popular scrapbooking app) in which she had archived online her favorite garden images. This will, of course, be of great anthropological interest to that child. Imagine instead that the child stumbles upon her grandmother's garden scrapbook, in which favorite images had been cut and pasted into compositions. Then I think she has stumbled onto a key to her grandmother's heart. One is a reference; the other an artifact. One is social; the other private. One is interesting; the other poignant. Why? The answer I think is the human hand. The eye and the hand and heart work together on a scrapbook to create meaning.

In creating a scrapbook, one is attempting to give shape to the things in the world one loves. It is implicit that this object itself is temporal, destined to either to be looked after and cherished, or maybe left to perish in a basement. The online scrapbook has no such destiny. It will live forever on the Internet with the potential to be shared by millions.

Scrapbooking is indeed a reliquary: an affirmation of what is beautiful in life and an offering to the future. Thankfully there are people like Charlotte Moss who lie in bed in the evening with scissors and glue and beloved bits of imagery producing these tender and very human works of art.

Deborah Needleman

BEYOND THE HORIZON

There is a certain madness that comes over one at the mere sight of a good map. —*Freya Stark* Nothing was so suited to African exploration as a good, thick skirt. —*Mary Kingsley* When you travel around the world, you must look and see; many people look but they do not see. They are always worried about the time of their flight, that the food is weird. They should forget such things and just get on and enjoy traveling and try to learn something new. —*Paul Smith* To travel is to write. —*Proust* The motorcar has restored the romance of travel. Freeing us from all the compulsions and contracts of the railway, the bondage to fixed hours and beaten tract, the approach to each town through the area of ugliness and desolation created by the railway itself, it has given us back the wonder, the adventure, and the novelty . . . these recovered pleasures must be ranked the delight of taking a town unawares, stealing on it by back ways . . . surprising in it some intimate aspect of past time . . . —*Edith Wharton* Thanks to the Interstate Highway System, it is now possible to travel from coast to coast without seeing anything. —*Charles Kuralt* . . . The postmasters in small towns read all the postcards. —*H. L. Mencken to George Jean Nathan* I will build a motorcar for the great multitude . . . But it will be so low in price that no man making a good salary will be unable to own one—and enjoy with his family the blessing of hours of pleasure in God's great open spaces. —*Henry Ford* I never travel without my diary; one should always have something sensational to read in the train. —*Oscar Wilde* Your mind must be like radar. To keep on and on on on. —*Henri Cartier-Bresson*

PARIS

Paris to the stranger is a way of living, a nostalgia, an essential element of human experience, poetry itself, and those who try to isolate her magic find that words become meaningless and adjectives lose their value, put to flight by the mysterious witchery which rises from the banks of the Seine.

Evangeline Bruce

PARIS IS POETRY

This is Paris.

In Paris, the present blends with the past as smoothly as a delicate sauce. Wandering streets where cars are often invisible, music can be heard coming from the neighborhood *école* while wafts of fresh baked bread lure you. You can almost envision a carriage about to turn the corner . . . This is Paris. Walking a few more steps, the corner reveals a bustling boulevard of automobiles heading in two different directions; a shop window reveals sleek leather chairs and glass tables; a woman is dressed in tall leather boots that seem one with her tall legs; there are others--in short skirts, tights, fur wraps--all with sunglasses and large bags slung over their shoulders, some accompanied by animals, some by men. Small groups of people sip coffee and chatter perched on woven seats appropriate for warm weather. It is January, and all seems like an outdoor party.

THIS IS Paris.

Farther on, a bookstore spills onto the street and passersby stop for a browse, perhaps a postcard or their next "read," a few magazines for the train. This is Paris. In the distance my eye catches a flower shop, plants, and trees outside in shapes you would only see on Parisian streets in January—anytime, for that matter. The condensation on the shop window allows a partial view inside. Intrigued, I open the door, and as if someone grabbed my hand, the fragrance invited me in. This is Paris. Tuberose wrapped and in hand, I head back to my hotel to install my indoor garden.
This is Paris.

Histoire de Paris

Les bouquinistes de la Seine

Le terme de "boucquain", sans doute dérivé du flamand "boeckjin" ou petit livre, fait son apparition en 1459, attesté sous la forme "bouquin" vers la fin du XVIe siècle. Dans son "Dictionnaire" de 1690, Furetière en donne la définition de "vieux livre fripé et peu connu" ; le vocable de bouquiniste désigne, quant à lui, depuis 1752, les marchands installés sur les quais. En effet, leurs boîtes investissent peu à peu les parapets, d'abord sur la rive gauche ; environ 300 sous la Révolution, ils connaissent une première réglementation grâce à l'ordonnance du 31 octobre 1822. Un premier recensement officiel en 1857 en dénombre 68 et le décret du 10 octobre 1859 consacre leur maintien, un temps menacé par les grands travaux d'Haussmann. Depuis 1891, ces "marchands d'esprit" ont l'autorisation de laisser sur place leurs caissons scellés pour la nuit. Selon Pierre Mac Orlan, ils représentent "le symbole de l'invitation aux voyages immobiles".

4e Arrᵗ

QUAI
DE
L'HÔTEL DE VILLE

The Man of Property

AGATHA CHRISTIE

MALMAISON

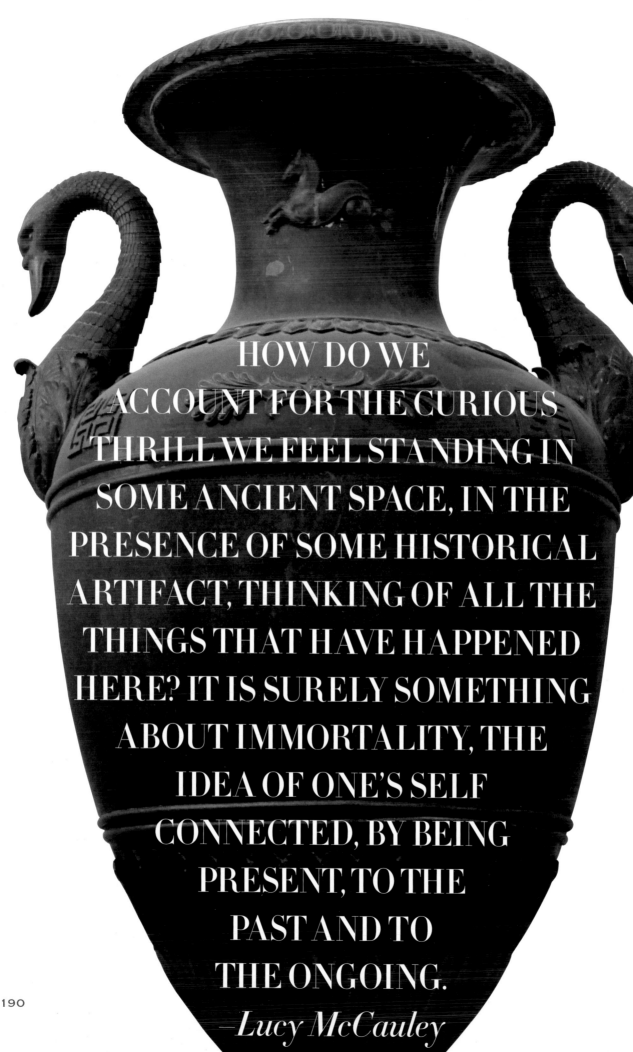

HOW DO WE
ACCOUNT FOR THE CURIOUS
THRILL WE FEEL STANDING IN
SOME ANCIENT SPACE, IN THE
PRESENCE OF SOME HISTORICAL
ARTIFACT, THINKING OF ALL THE
THINGS THAT HAVE HAPPENED
HERE? IT IS SURELY SOMETHING
ABOUT IMMORTALITY, THE
IDEA OF ONE'S SELF
CONNECTED, BY BEING
PRESENT, TO THE
PAST AND TO
THE ONGOING.
—*Lucy McCauley*

COURANCE

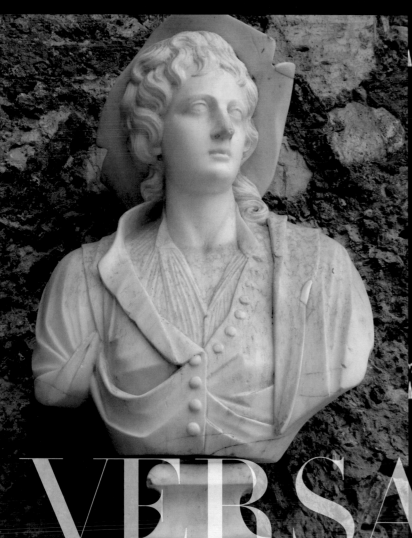

VERSAILLES

PLAN DE VERSAILLES,
DU PETIT PARC, ET DE SES DEPENDANCES
où sont marqués les emplacemens de chaque maison de cette Ville
les Plans du Château, et des Hôtels,
et les distributions des jardins et bosquets
Par M.r l'Abbé DELAGRIFE
Geographe de la Ville de Paris et de la Société Royale de Londres
M.DCC.XLVI

PLACE
D'ARMES

CAMP DES
FAINEANS

GRAND TRIANON

THE QUEEN'S HAMLET

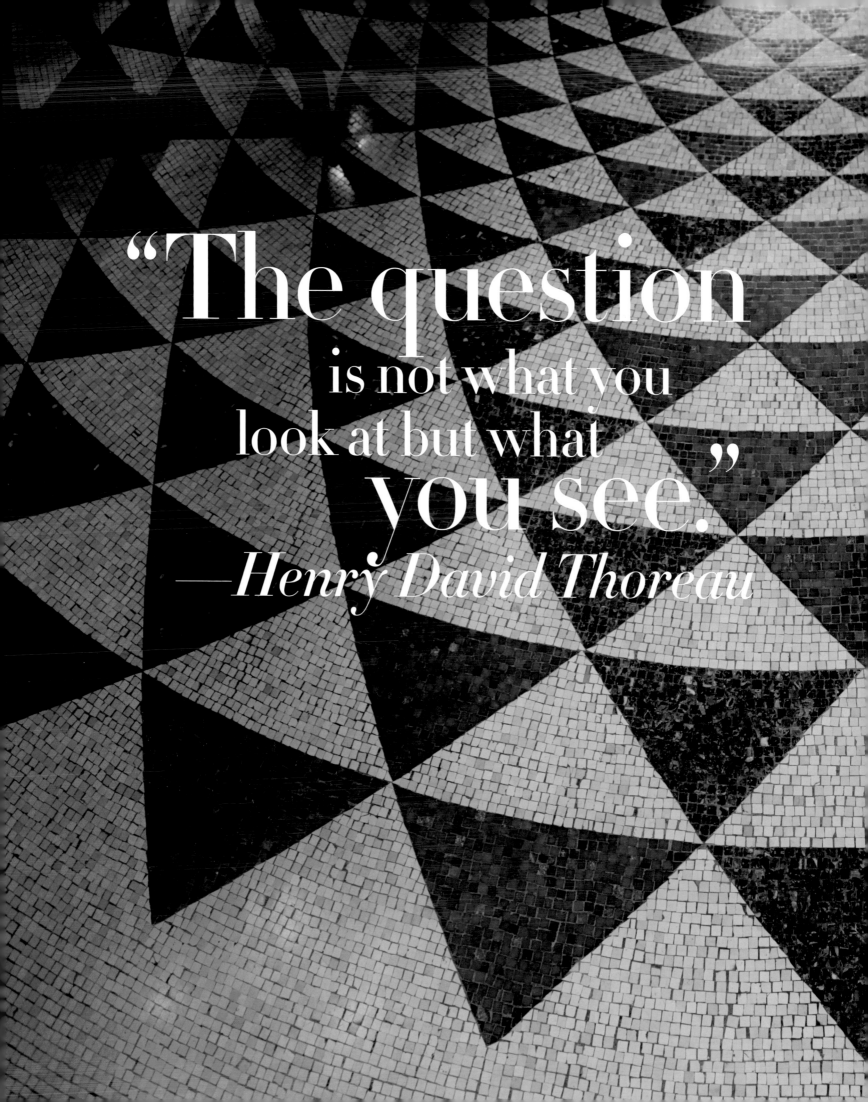

"The question is not what you look at but what you see."
—Henry David Thoreau

VILLA KERYLOS

BASTIDE
DE MARIE

La Bastide de Marie

...redi 4 Juillet 2008

...mpérature Prévue / Forecast Temperature

BALBIANELLO

VILLA
FELTRINELLI

Traveling is the ruin
of all happiness!
There's no looking
at a building here
after seeing Italy.
—*Fanny Burney*

VILLA GABRIELE
D'ANNUNZIO

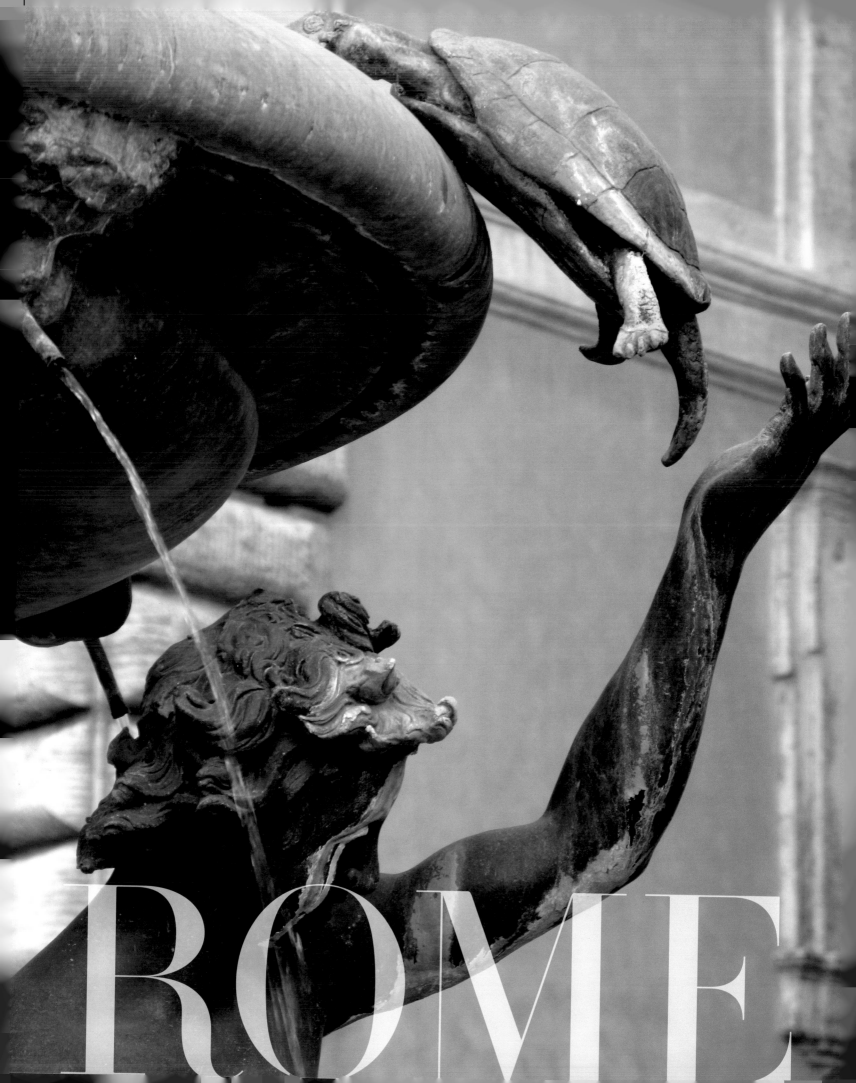

ROME

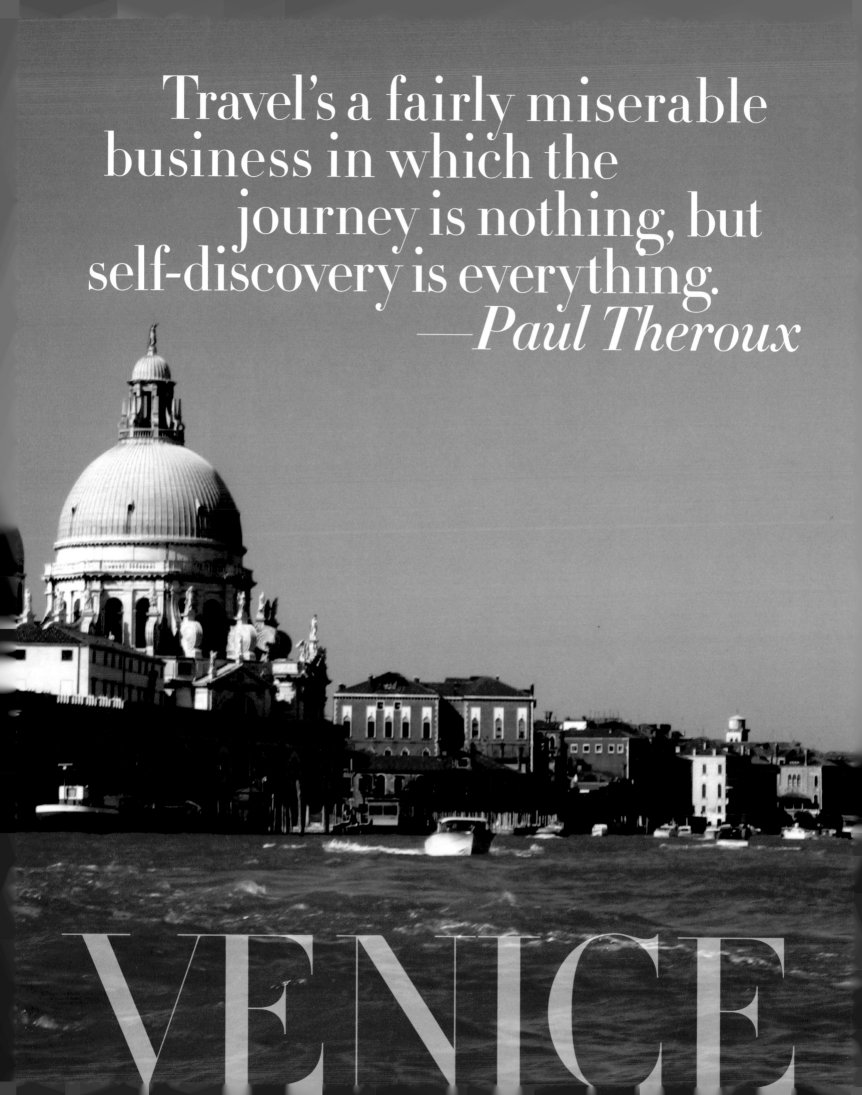

Travel's a fairly miserable business in which the journey is nothing, but self-discovery is everything.
—*Paul Theroux*

VENICE

VILLA D'ESTE

VILLA D'ESTE
LAGO DI COMO

EGYPT

ALREADY
I WANT
THE NEXT
THING.
—*Gertrude
Bell*

Setting out early from Edfu on Saturday morning we left the town with a thin haze of smoke settling on the rooftops. The night before we took an evening tour of the temple, only fifty of us . . . We seemed to have been absorbed into the vast sandstone walls as if figures incised like the myriad hieroglyphics . . . Forty-two meters high and walls decorated from bottom to top, it is hard to imagine the scale and the extent and intricacy of the hiero- glyphics, from approximately 1.5 inches to life size. A half moon peering out from behind sinister evening clouds, as if reminding us of the rituals conducted and an afterlife prayed and planned for. The riverbanks in between villages and towns are lined with palms and papyrus. Clusters of lotus float by with large lavender colored blossoms and an egret resting mid Nile. Cows graze, boys fish, men farm small plots at the rivers edge or squat under fragile structures composed of discarded palm fronds. Some young boys trot along on donkeys, others washing clothes in the Nile, as if nothing has changed since Moses.

"One night in December, a man decided to leave his house and his vineyards, his work of translating Elizabethan poets into French, to spend two months in a country unfamiliar to him. He and his wife would leave for Russia the day after Christmas, and return in March.

They were in the habit of taking long trips together … They chose winter because of all seasons it is the most Russian. Winter is a season for Russians alone …"
—Pauline de Rothschild
(*The Irrational Journey*)

RUSSIA

BEYOND
THE HORIZON

My wanderlust began in earnest when I took my first trip to Europe in October 1967. It was utter happenstance—a tale too long and complicated to tell here. Suffice it to say that as a young woman in my early twenties, who'd traveled no farther than Southern California, had taken a grand total of four flights, and had never lived away from home, I found myself on a transatlantic ship crossing the Atlantic from New York to Naples. (I pinched myself so often I almost turned black and blue.) Other than living somewhere in Italy, I was without a clear itinerary and not at all sure how long I'd stay—a week, a month, a year, forever? It was, I suppose, my own version of *Eat, Pray, Love*, sans the psychodrama.

From the moment I boarded the ship, I began to take notes about every memorable moment. I've been taking notes ever since; it's a habit that I have no intention of breaking. From Naples, I went straight to Rome for a few days, then to Florence, where I decided to base myself. It was a snap decision, no regrets. As I traveled to other countries, I kept a journal, mailed postcards home (which my family kept and returned to me), and recorded every detail—meals eaten, excursions made, people met. Little did I know it would be excellent preparation for what would become my first job in journalism: working for a travel magazine. In fact, my experience traveling alone in Europe was probably the reason I was hired.

Now, forty some years later, I have boxes of journals—many of them the basis for articles I wrote for *Holiday*, *Travel & Leisure*, and *Town & Country*, my alma maters. My most trusty companions are what are called "reporter's notebooks," eight-by-four-inch spiral-bound pads of seventy lined sheets and plenty of non-leaky pens. The pad is narrow enough to fit snugly in one hand while I write with the other and small enough to carry. It's long been the essential accoutrement for reporters (hence, the name). Nowadays, many journalists have traded in their notebooks for laptops or tape recorders. Not I. Suppose you're stuck on an atoll in the Pacific with no electricity. Try powering up.

I don't keep a diary and never did, but there's something about taking a trip that compels me to memorialize it as it occurs or soon thereafter. It's a way to capture the experience, to bottle it for perpetuity so that no one and nothing can take it

away (unless, of course, you lose it; don't!). Writers have been doing this for centuries. Think of the travel essays of Edith Wharton, Nathaniel Hawthorne, Henry James, and Goethe, D. H. Lawrence, John Steinbeck, Lawrence Durrell, and Eric Newby—not to mention the logs and diaries of such eminent explorers as Marco Polo, Charles Darwin, Captain James Cook, Sir Richard Burton, T. E. Lawrence, Mark Twain, and Alexis de Tocqueville. Their counterparts today—Paul Theroux, Peter Mayle, William Least Heat-Moon, Bill Bryson, Jan Morris, Frances Mayes, Elizabeth Gilbert, and the late Bruce Chatwin—have carried on the tradition with gusto.

Not all of the entries of those early diarists were scintillating. Edith Wharton went on her first trip to Europe with her parents when she was only four, so she was no stranger to foreign travel. Though her early writings were plodding ("And then we went . . ."), she got better, much better, and more insightful. In her essay "Taste," in *French Ways and Their Meaning*, she writes: "The artistic integrity of the French has led them to feel from the beginning that there is no difference in kind between the curve of a woman's hat brim and the curve of a Rodin marble, or between the droop of an upholsterer's curtain and that of the branches along a great avenue laid out by Le Nôtre."

Nomadic females like Lesley Blanch (*The Wilder Shores of Love*), Rebecca West (*Black Lamb and Grey Falcon*), Beryl Markham (*West with the Night*), Freya Stark (*A Winter in Arabia*), and Karen Blixen aka Isak Dinesen (*Out of Africa*) fed the fantasies of many women (and men, too), instilling in us curiosity and courage about what might lie around the corner and beyond the horizon.

Speaking of horizons, consider the enduring images certain artists have etched in our minds with their observations of Venice (Turner), Provence (van Gogh), and the Côte d'Azur and Morocco (Matisse). Mention the word "Tahiti," and inevitably the voluptuous sarong-clad beauties portrayed by Paul Gauguin leap to mind. Illustrators such as Ludwig Bemelmans, Saul Steinberg, Ronald Searle, and Pierre Le-Tan beckoned us to journey with them through their felicitous line drawings and watercolors.

Photographers, too, have allowed us to follow in their footsteps. Ansel Adams took us to the American West, especially Yosemite National Park, in black and white. Henri Cartier-Bresson made us want to trail behind the little French boy carrying the baguette on the back of his *bicyclette* through the French countryside. In fact, HCB, as he was known, kept a scrapbook of his photographs squirreled away on a shelf in his parents' home in Normandy. He forgot where he placed them. Years later, they were discovered. It was akin to coming upon a trunk full of treasures.

On the luxurious side, Slim Aarons seduced us with sun-soaked images of the glamorous playgrounds of St. Tropez, Gstaad, Marbella, Acapulco, and Barbados. Perpetually suntanned, Slim would return from an assignment, sunglasses perched on

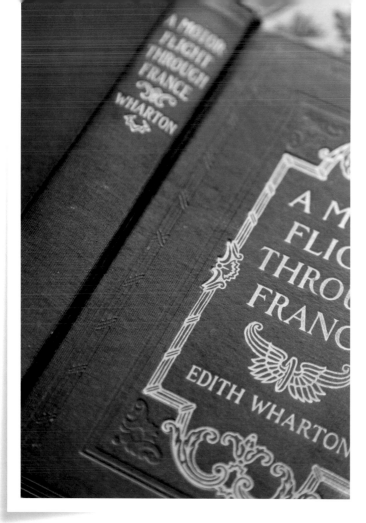

his head and a carousel of 35mm slides under his arm, ready to regale his editors at *Holiday* magazine and later at *Town & Country* with stories of his jet-set subjects as he did his show-and-tell in the screening room. Those of us lucky to be present were in his thrall and not a little envious.

In the past, I rarely traveled with a camera—too cumbersome and often too heavy. It was a burden. Now, with lightweight digital cameras and smartphones that take pictures (good ones, too), it's a snap—literally. My latest trip was a three-day mission with UNICEF to Haiti to see the progress after the devastating earthquake in 2010. Between my little Sony digital and my BlackBerry, I was able to take images that are both riveting and publishable. And I love being able to email them.

When my husband accompanies me, he takes most of the pictures (and is much better at it than I). Upon our return home, he'll immediately download them on his computer with the purpose of creating a book. It's the high-tech version of an old-fashioned photo album and, even better, can be ordered in multiples (they make wonderful gifts, by the way, particularly if you took the trip with friends or family).

All such renderings—whether written or painted, photographed or digitized—keep the memories of others vividly alive for the rest of us to dream about. They may even stimulate us to go off on our own. In 1951, two sisters, aged eighteen and twenty-two, took their first trip to Europe together. They traveled to London, Paris, Venice, Rome, and Florence. The result: an utterly fetching collection of handwritten notes, poetry, fanciful sketches, and drawings called *One Special Summer*. The girls were none other than Jacqueline Bouvier (later Jackie Kennedy Onassis) and her sister, who would become Lee Radziwill—two of the most beautiful and spirited young women who ever were. For me, One Special Summer is a model of what a travel scrapbook should be—light-hearted, episodic, and brimming with exuberance.

Unlike a carefully crafted essay or oil painting, a scrapbook is more random (seemingly) and looser—a composite rather than a composition. I've always envied people who keep them because a great deal of work and artistry are required. The result is a gathering of impressions, textures, and mediums—part diary, part sketchbook, and highly personal. A scrapbook needn't be one dimensional either: it can contain mementos such as pressed flowers or leaves, matchbook covers, menus, invitation, place cards, snapshots, souvenirs, doodles, and textiles. In its own revealing way, a scrapbook serves as a kind of elevated Rorschach test for travelers. Page through one and you're bound to discover something about the journey, but you'll also learn something about the journeyer. Does she have a predilection for gardens or statuary? Is he fixated on architecture or ancient ruins? Maybe the traveler finds the human face and figure more to his or her liking or is drawn to the loneliness of empty rooms and deserted landscapes. Nature lovers might focus on sunsets, sunrises, and the four seasons. Whatever the preferences, the effect sheds light on who this person is—or desires to be. Travel, after all, is about heightened experiences, not about daily life. Paul Theroux once wrote: "I decided that travel was flight and pursuit in equal parts." Expectations are high—the search is on for some place different, something not found at home. Otherwise, why go away at all?

One of my favorite travel diaries is *Italian Journey* by Johann Wolfgang von Goethe. Between 1786 and 1788, the protean Goethe not only wrote about Italy but also sketched and painted it. Toward the end of his wanderings in the south, he reflects on what he has seen: "Now that my mind is stored with images of all these coasts and promontories, gulfs and bays, islands and headlands, rocky cliffs and sandy beaches, wooded hills and gentle pastures, fertile fields, flower gardens, tended trees, festooned vines, mountains wreathed in clouds, eternally serene plains and the all-encircling sea with its ever-changing colors and moods, for the first time the *Odyssey* has become a living truth to me." I daresay Homer couldn't have said it better himself.

Artists sketch, paint, and sculpt. Writers jot, scribble, type, erase, and scribble again. Designers talk, gesticulate, research, pray, and sketch, and any combination of the above, over and over again. Often times designers cull images, fragments, swatches, photos, and bits and pieces and assemble them onto a storyboard, a collage, a three-dimensional collective conscious of material that represents a thread of thought--an emotion, a place they want you to feel connected to, a place perhaps they want to transport you to. Whatever the vehicle--camera, sketchbook, iPad, chalkboard--when the idea lands via brush or pen it is then giving shape and meaning to all the thinking, musing, and wondering that has been stirring for some indeterminate period that may seem like a lifetime, and might in fact be a month, a week, or a moment.

The rooms of Valentino,
Hubert de Givenchy,
John Richardson, and
others too numerous to
list, are living in
my files for reference.
Amazing, isn't it,
how one picture can
say so much?

Remember your first kaleidoscope? All those colors thrashing around
in unison--didn't they all seem to go together? Then, at some
point, we developed opinions about "what goes" and "what doesn't."
Later on, we went through another phase where those theories
collapsed and we became more open-minded and relaxed in our
choices. Ah, choices--liberation from rules. The choice is yours.
The following pages are color stories waiting to happen. I've done
them for a reason. Some MUST be in MY future--maybe yours, too?

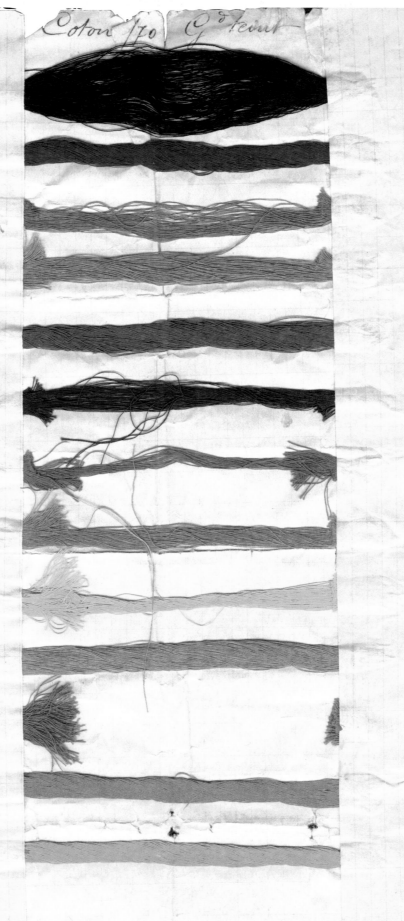

150 G:562	2ᵏ00
Bleu 158 G:562	0.100
Ciel 42 G:ᴸ562	1.200
Ciel 42 G:548	0.250
Gris 84 G:562	0.600
Jade G:562	0.120
Nil 32 G:466	0.120
...usse G:562	0.020
Or 10 G:562	0.010
Beige 124 G:562	0.700
Poivre 100 G:503	0.050
Beige 66 G:562	0.950
Rose 41 G:466	0.920

"In 1992, Ebrahim Mukhtari made a documentary called *Saffron* about a month in the life of the villagers of Bajestan, 500 kilometers south of Mashhad. What had touched him most about saffron, he said . . . was the fragility of the process: the delicacy of placing the corms into that rugged land, the way they open for one day only, and the brittleness of the little dried threads."
— Victoria Finlay

I have memories of green . . . Brush-Everard Green in Colonial Williamsburg, the floor of the Octagon room at Monticello, the *mintiness* of the Hermitage Museum . . . BUT, the fragrant memories are the ones that return often: the flower shop that I would visit long ago with its brick floor always wet and partially hidden by stems and petals. As you walked, the crunching and snapping of discarded stems released a cacophony of green notes with an occasional waft of lilac or tuberose, but it was the sweet and pungent greens that seduced me . . . the ivies mixed with box, chrysanthemum stems crushed against scented geranium, and the gentleness of verbena. Green is a perfume to me.

You might

be surprised

COLLECTION
LES
BEAUX-PAY

COLLECTION
LES
BEAUX PAYS

—

GABRIELLE
RÉVAL

PIERRE BOF

Collection
Les
Belles
Rivières
de France

AVIGNON
AU
DOUBLE
VISAGE

COLLECTION
LES
BEAUX

René Cuzac

MARCE

L'Adour

PROVENCE

ET

ES GAVE

6

decorate

"This pale pink reminds me of opals and pearls, Jean Harlow and silk charmeuse, 'New Dawn' roses and a baby's rosy cheeks. Who wouldn't want a perpetual glow like that? When it comes to decorating, it's perfect with black and white and everything in between. And real men do like pink—they just might not admit it at first!"

CHARLOTTE MOSS

PANTONE 705-C

0,85 € FRANCE

LA POSTE 2008

Les globes de Coronelli

CONTRIBUTORS

DEEDA BLAIR

Deeda Blair is a long-standing advocate for biomedical research and for advancing global public health. Mrs. Blair served for thirty-five years as Vice President of the Albert and Mary Lasker Foundation. Mrs. Blair has been involved since 1982 with the Harvard School of Public Health. She is Co-Chairman of the Harvard AIDS Initiative International Advisory Council and is a member of the Harvard AIDS Initiative Policy Board. Having lived in Asia and Europe as the wife of Ambassador William McCormick Blair, Jr., she became deeply interested in a global approach to the prevention and treatment of infectious diseases. Mrs. Blair has been Secretary and a director of the Foundation for the National Institute of Health since its inception fifteen years ago and served on the Board of Scripps Research Institute. Mrs. Blair has also served for more than twelve years on the Board of the American Cancer Society.

ALEXA HAMPTON

Alexa Hampton, president and owner of Mark Hampton, LLC and Alexa Hampton, Inc., her NY-based interior and product design firms, specializes in classical, traditional and eclectic residential and commercial interior and home furnishings design. Nationally recognized, most recently by AD as one of their AD 100 since 2002, Hampton's interiors are known to be refined with an international influence. Among many of her active roles within the industry, Hampton has published the successful design book, *The Language of Interior Design* (Clarkson Potter, 2010) and writes a regular design column for the "Off Duty" section of the Wall Street Journal.

PIETER ESTERSOHN

Pieter Estersohn began working at *Interview* magazine when he was nineteen. He is now a frequent contributor to *Elle Decor*, *Martha Stewart Living*, and other leading lifestyle magazines. His photographs have also appeared in many interior design books, including *Charlotte Moss Decorates* (Rizzoli, 2011), *Charlotte Moss: A Flair For Living* (Assouline, 2008), *At Home* (Rizzoli, 2010), *Recipes for Parties* (Rizzoli, 2010), *Walls* (Rizzoli, 2011), and many more.

PAMELA FIORI

Pamela Fiori's career in magazine publishing spans more than forty years. She was editor-in-chief of *Town & Country* for seventeen years, and before that, she served as editor-in-chief of *Travel & Leisure* for fourteen years. An authority on luxury, travel, style, connoisseurship, and philanthropy, Fiori writes and speaks frequently on these subjects. Her first book, *Stolen Moments*, is a tribute to the photography of Ronny Jaques, a contemporary of Richard Avedon and Lillian Bassman. She has also written *In the Spirit of Capri* (Assouline, 2009), *In the Spirit of St. Barths* (Assouline, 2011), *At the Table at Le Cirque* (Rizzoli, 2012), and *In the Spirit of Palm Beach* (Assouline, 2012).

DEBORAH NEEDLEMAN

Deborah Needleman is the editor-in-chief of WSJ Magazine, the Wall Street Journal's luxury monthly, and the creator of "Off Duty," the Journal's Saturday lifestyle section, which she continues to oversee. In 2005, she launched *domino* magazine as its founding editor-in-chief. Needleman's writing on style, design and gardens has appeared in *The New York Times*, *Slate*, *House & Garden* and *The Huffington Post*. She was editor-at-large for *House & Garden*, and started her career as photography editor of *The Washington Post Magazine*. She is co-author of New York Times bestseller *The Domino Book of Decorating* (Simon & Schuster, 2008) and author of *The Perfectly Imperfect Home* (Clarkson Potter, 2011). She lives in Manhattan with her husband, Jacob Weisberg, and their two children.

CANDY PRATTS PRICE

Candy Pratts Price is the editor-at-large for Vogue.com. She is the recipient of many awards and is also a frequent television guest and has appeared on many programs, including *Good Morning America*, *The Today Show*, *CBS Early Show*, *Fashion Television*, and more. In 2003, she curated the exhibition "Manolo Blahnik . . . The Shoe: A Celebration of Design," a historical retrospective of the world's most famous shoe designer. In 2008, Pratts Price edited the definitive publication *American Fashion Accessories*. She is also well known for her popular video series "CandyCast" on Vogue.com. A native of New York City, Candy Pratts Price is a graduate of FIT and former faculty member at Parsons School of Design.

RESOURCES

RECOMMENDED SCRAPBOOKING SUPPLIES

GLUE STICKS
Avery
Best-Test rubber cement
OIC Precision Glue Stick
Quickie glue (Pinpoint roller for gluing down edges...and tiny things)
SCOTCH (Wrinkle-free gluestick)

SCISSORS
Fiskars
Maped Crea Cut Scissors (five interchangeable blades for varying trim patterns)
Precision Sandkaulen pinking shears
Westcott Scissors

NATIONAL CHAINS

Ben Franklin
www.benfranklinstores.com

Burnes of Boston
www.burnes.com

CR Gibson
www.crgibson.com

Creative Memories
www.creativememories.com

Exposures Online
www.exposuresonline.com

Hobby Lobby
www.hobbylobby.com

Jam Paper
www.jampaper.com

Jo-Ann Fabric and Craft
www.joann.com

Lee's Art Supply
www.leesartshop.com

Martha Stewart
www.marthastewart.com

Michael's Craft Store
www.michaels.com

NY Central Art Supply
www.nycentralart.com

Paper Source
www.paper-source.com

Papyrus
www.papyrusonline.com

Sam Flax
www.samflax.com

Scrapbook.com
www.store.scrapbook.com

The Container Store
www.containerstore.com

BOUTIQUES AND SPECIALTY STORES

VOGEL
FINE BINDINGS

The Vogel Bindery
Paul Vogel, Bookbinder
(631) 329-3106
www.vogelbindery.com
For custom leather scrapbooks, boxes, journals & more.

Kinsey Marable & Co.
www.privatelibraries.com
Booksellers and furnishers of distinctive private libraries.

ATLANTA
Paces Papers, Inc., by Jackie
Cates Center
110 East Andrews Drive
Atlanta, Georgia 30305
(404) 231-1111
www.pacespapers.com

DALLAS
Bell'Invito
1403 Dragon Street
Dallas, TX 75207
(214) 741-1717
www.bellinvito.com

HOUSTON
PH Design Shop
2414 Rice Boulevard
Houston, TX 77005
(713) 522-8861
www.phdesignshop.com

LOS ANGELES
Soolip Paperie
548 Norwich Drive
West Hollywood, CA 90048
(310) 360-0545
www.soolip.com

Pulp
456 S. La Brea Avenue
Los Angeles, CA 90036
(323) 937-3505

NEW YORK
The Ink Pad
37 7th Avenue
New York, NY 10014
(212) 463-9876
www.theinkpadnyc.com

Greenwich Letterpress
39 Christopher Street
New York, NY 10014
(212) 989-7464
www.greenwichletterpress.com

Paper Presentations
23 W. 18th Street
New York, NY 10011
(212) 463-7035
www.paperpresentations.com

Sennelier
3 Quai Voltaire
75007 Paris 07, France
+33 01 42 60 72 15
www.magasinsennelier.com

SAN FRANCISCO
Bell'occhio
10 Brady Street
San Francisco, CA 94103
(415) 864-4048
www.bellocchio.com

ONLINE SPECIALTY STORES

A Favorite Design for quote cards
www.afavoritedesign.com

Knock Knock Stuff for funny
and clever items
www.knockknockstuff.com

Lunalux
www.lunalux.com

Oblation Papers.com for
journals and cards
www.oblationpapers.com

GOING DIGITAL . . .

SOFTWARE FOR DIGITAL SCRAPBOOKING:
Adobe Creative Suite
(Photoshop, InDesign, Illustrator)

FOR SOCIAL MEDIA SCRAPBOOKERS:
Pinterest
www.pinterest.com
Polyvore
www.polyvore.com

SCRAPBOOKING AND COLLAGE APPS
FROM THE APPLE STORE:
Collage
iScrapbook

LetterMPress
My Memory Suite
ScrapPad
Scatter

BOOK CREATION RESOURCES
Apple/iPhoto
www.apple.com

Blurb
www.blurb.com

Creative Memories
www.creativememories.com

Lulu
www.lulu.com

My Publisher
www.mypublisher.com

Shutterfly
www.shutterfly.com

HELPFUL BLOGS AND WEBSITES
www.addictedtoscrapbooking.com
www.creatingkeepsakes.com
blogs.creativememories.com
www.internationalcollage.org
www.writeclickscrapbook.com

GARDEN FAVORITES

Château d'Ainay le Vieil
Rue Drevant
18200 Ainay-le-Vieil, France
+33 2 48 63 36 14
chateau-ainaylevieil.fr
chateau-ainaylevieil.fr/contact

Chateau de Courances
Rue du Château
91490 COURANCES
33 01.64.98.07.36
www.courances.net
info@courances.net

Château de Gourdon
Place Château
06620 Gourdon, France
+33 4 93 09 68 02
chateau-gourdon.com
contact@chateau-gourdon.com

Château de Hautefort
Le Bourg d'Hautefort
24390 Hautefort, France
+33 5 53 50 51 23
www.chateau-hautefort.com
contact@chateau-hautefort.com

Château de Losse
24290 Thonac, France
+33 5 53 50 80 08
www.chateaudelosse.com/en
chateaudelosse24@yahoo.fr

Château de Marqueyssac
24220 Vézac, France
+33 5 53 31 36 36
www.marqueyssac.com
jardins@marqueyssac.com

Château de Talcy
18 Rue du Château
41370 Talcy, France
+33 2 54 81 03 01
talcy.monuments-nationaux.fr/en
www.monuments-nationaux.fr/en/
contact/monument-s-contacts/

Gardens of Eyrignac
Eyrignac,
24590 Salignac-Eyvigues, France
+33 5 53 28 99 71
www.eyrignac.com
contact@eyrignac.com

HOTEL FAVORITES

Castel Monastero
Monastero D'Ombrone, 19
53109 Castelnuovo Berardenga –
Siena Italy
+39 070 9218222
www.castelmonastero.com

Four Seasons Hotels and Resorts
91 Locations Worldwide
www.fourseasons.com

Hotel Cipriani
Piazza Santa Fosca 29
30142 Torcello, Venezia Italy
+39 041 730150
www.locandacipriani.com
info@locandacipriani.com

Hotel du Cap-Eden-Roc
Boulevard JF Kennedy
06601 Antibes, France
+33 (0)4 93 61 39 01
www.hotel-du-cap-eden-roc.com/
eng/welcome/
reservation@hdcer.com

La Bastide de Marie
Route de Bonnieux Quartier de la
Verrerie
84560 Ménerbes France
+33 (0)4 57 74 74 74
www.labastidedemarie.com
epiriou@groupe-sibuet.com

La Pinede St. Tropez
Plage de Bouillabaisse
83990 Saint-Tropez, France
+33 4 94 55 91 00
www.residencepinede.com
reservation@residencepinede.com

Le Dokhan's Hotel
117 Rue de Lauriston
75116 Paris, France
+33 01 536 56699
www.radissonblu.com/
dokhanhotel-paristrocadero

Le Meurice, Paris
228 Rue de Rivoli
75001 Paris, France
+33 01 44 58 1010
www.lemeurice.com

Le Vieux Logis, Hotel
Rue des écoles
24510 Trémolat, France
+33 (0)5 53 22 80 06
www.vieux-logis.com/uk/index.php
vieuxlogis@relaischateaux.com

Mandarin Oriental Paris
251 Rue Saint-Honoré
75001 Paris, France
+33 01 70 98 7878
www.mandarinoriental.com/paris

Prieuré Notre-Dame d'Orsan
Prieuré d'Orsan
18170 Maisonnais
+ 33 02 48 56 27 50
www.prieurdorsan.com

St. Regis Hotels and Resorts
44 Locations Worldwide
www.starwoodhotels.com/stregis

The Bauer Venezia
S. Marco 1459
30124 Venice, Italy
+39 0 41 520 7022
www.bauervenezia.com

The Ritz Paris
15 Place Vendôme
75001 Paris, France
+33 0 1 43 16 3030
www.ritzparis.com

Villa D'Este
Via Regina, 40
22012 Cernobbio Italy
+39 031.3481
www.villadeste.com/en/34/
location.aspx
reservations@villadeste.it

Villa Feltrinelli
Via Rimembranza, 38
25084 Gargnano Brescia, Italy
(+39) 0365 798000
www.villafeltrinelli.com
booking@villafeltrinelli.com

OTHER PRODUCTS BY CHARLOTTE MOSS

Framed art for Soicher Marin
www.Soicher-Marin.com

Furniture for Century Icons
www.centuryfurniture.com/icons

Fabrics for Fabricut
www.Fabricut.com

Rugs, Sisal Carpeting & Scenic Mural
Wallcoverings for Stark Carpet
www.StarkCarpet.com

China for Pickard
www.PickardChina.com

Fabrics & Wallcoverings for
Brunschwig & Fils
www.Brunschwig.com

Please visit
www.CharlotteMoss.com

ACKNOWLEDGMENTS

Between these two covers is the work of a number of people. In fact, I am always reminded when writing this page in each book just HOW MANY people it takes to do a book like this. Directly, indirectly, in whole, or in part, moral support, and every other type you could imagine, there are many people to thank.

First, I would like to thank my husband, Barry, as I am always thanking him last, and he more than anyone has LIVED with the book, talk of the book, the deadlines, the blocks, the drafts, the frustrations, but also the gratification and exhilaration that comes with THE END. Thank you.

To Matthew Kowles my right hand and chief organizer through it all . . . staying on top of deadlines, photo shoots and photo logs, permissions, meetings, and on and on . . . and for doing it calmly and always the gentleman. Thank you.

To Ali Power, my editor who walked with me through this process, understood my vision—that photos and text were both part of my collage method and how some photos require NO words and so much more. Even when I was woefully behind, she remained calm but firm, this book honestly would not be in your hands right now if it were not for her steady support of me and this project.

To Isabel Venero, my editorial champion on the subject from the very beginning, to Doug Turshen for art direction and patience, and Steve Turner for design.

To Phyllis Wender my agent for always believing in me and that I will always get it done (eventually) because there are other book ideas already in the works. BUT, "This one first, Char...." , "of course, PW . . ."

To my beautiful, talented, intelligent, elegant, and witty contributors . . . Pamela Fiori, Deeda Blair, Deborah Needleman, Candy Pratts Price, and Alexa Hampton. Each one of these ladies brings something unique to the subject. Their insights, knowledge, sense of history, and their sense of humor add to this book far beyond their words. I am deeply grateful for their contribution and for believing in the subject, but even more so for their friendship.

To Pieter Estersohn . . . not only for his beautiful photos but also for the fun we have on shoots, talking about life, books, travel . . . getting the RIGHT shot, and of course, always fun meals together.

To Eric Strifler for his photos, his persistence to 'get the shot,' his dry sense of humor, and for being such a great team player.

To everyone who works for me at home for all the things they do to keep it all going—and most of the time without me knowing it is happening. To Sean McNally with Wilma Liebman, Maria Ebeuna, and Eddie Pabon in New York. Without them I could not function. Meals, flowers, pick-ups and deliveries, and otherwise running behind me with the glasses, iphone or ipad I have managed to inevitably leave behind. In East Hampton, Gary Bohan, Inga Spring, and Jeimmy Gonzalez for all the same exact things . . . In Aspen, to Arcelia Torres and Guillermo for always having a perfectly calm house when we arrive for a visit or a shoot.

To Paul Vogel for his beautiful work: my leather scrapbooks, clippings boxes, all of the book binding for my out-of-print, or antique books. But what I appreciate most is his "anything can be done" attitude, his suggestions and advice. Visits to his studio always end up being great conversations with he and his wife Abby. I always come away with lessons on a technique, a new idea, or become inspired for a new project.

To Paul Myers-Davis in my office who has been responsible for the cataloging of thousands of photographs, from all of my trips, family vacations, wildflower hunts, the cataloging of my garden photos each weekend in the summer, and so much more, as evidenced by the photos in this book. In addition, Paul is responsible for our website maintenance, graphics, and the design of "C'est Inspire." And to Johanna Barger my assistant who is the pivot point between all of the above: the calendar, the events, the people, and an overwhelming mountain of detail.

To Daniel Murphy, paper artist extraordinaire, for his collage technique and inspiration. Learning something new is essential, always exciting, and our shared love of paper I am thrilled came together in this book.

To Victoria Molinelli for her beautiful portraits of my contributors. I love her style and how she captured everyone.

To Maryrose Grossman at the John F Kennedy Library in Boston for her research assistance with the White House flowers styled with Mrs. Kennedy's supervision.

To Keiki Jordan and Joan Adler for their custom work and needle wizardry and willingness to work on tight deadlines. To Rory Kotin of Scribe, Ink for all the beautiful calligraphy she has done for me over the years . . . invitations, place cards, menu cards, coat tags, gift tags . . . you name it, and all in that exquisite hand in divine colored inks.

To Mark Sanne and Jean Cuty-Peretz for all the meals they have prepared at home for parties and family affairs for four or forty, and always on time, no matter how many times I change it . . . and with a sense of humor.

PHOTOGRAPHY CREDITS

Tommy Agriodimas: 61 (*Top, left to right: Gloria Vanderbilt, Wendy Goodman, Richard Moyer, Liz O'Brien, Michael Raynes, Peter Speliopoulos, Robert Turner, David Meitus; Middle, left to right: Dr. Lauren Tancredi & Gloria Vanderbilt, Kitty Hawks, Ben Brantley, Wendy Goodman, Robert Ruffino; Bottom, left to right: Phyllis Stepp, Bill Stubbs, Nancy Biddle, Aurora Stokowski, Richard David Story*), 66–67, 68 (*Top, left to right: Charlotte Moss, Deb Shriver, Glenda Bailey, Charlotte Moss, Chris Taylor, Dayle Haddon; Middle, left to right: Deb Shriver, Jane Scott Hodges; Bottom, right: Glenda Bailey, Pamela Fiori*), 69 (*Middle, left: Ellen Levine, Stephen Drucker; Bottom, center: Dayle Haddon, Deb Shriver*); Dale Booher: 134, top (garden plan); Gary Bohan: 137 (watercolors); Louise Dahl-Wolfe, Pauline de Rothschild, 1940. Posthumous digital reproduction from original negative. Louise Dahl-Wolfe Archive, Center for Creative Photography, 1989 Arizona Board of Regents: 52; Original print by Robert Dash, 2011: 11; Pieter Estersohn: 8–15, 17, 19, 22–25, 28–31, 41 center, 42–48, 50–51, 56, 58–60, 71–72, 80 inset, 83–85, 87, 91, 94, 97, 105, 108–110, 113, 115, 117, 121–23, 232, 243 bottom right; Courtesy Hearst Publications: 49; Thibault Jeanson: 16 left, 57, 183; Porcelain and copper Hyacinth arrangement in 18 C. basket by Vladimir Kanevsky. Photo by Vladimir Kanevsky: 74; Knudsen, 1962. Courtesy of the JFK Memorial Library: 46; Patrick McMullan Inc.: 63–64, 65 (*Top, left to right: Ruth Wilkinson, Hutton Wilkinson, Hutton Wilkinson, Francesca Stanfill Nye, Keith Langham, Charlotte Moss*); portraits by Victoria Molinelli: 268-269, 271; Charlotte Moss: 1–7, 14 lower right, 16 right, 21, 27, 32, 35, 37–41, 49 background, 52–53, 72 (flowers), 73, 75, 77, 81–82, 92–93, 95–96, 98–99, 102, 104, 106–7, 111–2,118–9, 124–25, 130–31, 134–35, 136, 138–39, 140–45, 148–49, 152–53, 156–57, 160–62, 166–67, 170–71, 174–75, 178–79 insets, 181–82, 184–85, 187–89, 192–203, 206–221, 224, 228, 230, 233–39, 242 top right, 244–267, 270; photography by Charlotte Moss, collages by Daniel Murphy: 18, 146–47, 150–51, 154–55, 158–59, 164–65, 168–69, 172–73, 176–77, 190–91, 204–5, 222–23, 225–27; from the personal photo album of Elsie de Wolfe, courtesy of Charlotte Moss: 89; Eric Striffler: 34, 36, 78, 116 inset, 120, 126–27, 128 left, 132, 180, 241, 242 top left, 242 top right, 242 center, 242 bottom right, 243 top left, 243, center left, 272; Annie Schlechter: 86; Keith Scott Morton/House & Garden © The Condé Nast Publications Ltd.: 128; Max Sinsteden: 194, top left; Hannah Thomson: 55, top row, center row, bottom left, bottom right (*Top, center: Charlotte Moss;*

Center, left: Charlotte Moss, Ralph Rucci; Bottom, left to right: Andrew Bolton, Anna Sui, Emily Rafferty, Deeda Blair); Turner, Joseph Mallord William (1775-1851). *Venice, Suburb, Moon Rise.* Tate, London / Art Resource, NY: 242 bottom left; Simon Upton: 101,103

FABRICS:
Braquenie, Paris: 100; Brunschwig & Fils "Menars Border Cotton Print, Pompeian Red": 79, 90; hand-painted linen from the collection of Nancy Lancaster: 82; "Digby's Tent" by Charlotte Moss for Brunschwig & Fils: 114; "Ethel" by Charlotte Moss for Fabricut: 133; "Zarafa" by Charlotte Moss for Brunschwig & Fils: 186; Vintage textiles: 36, 37, 39, 48, 50-51, 52, 57, 70.

First published in the United States of America in 2012 by Rizzoli International Publications, Inc.
300 Park Avenue South
New York, NY 10010
www.rizzoliusa.com

© 2012 Charlotte Moss

2013 2014 2015 / 10 9 8 7 6 5 4 3 2

Printed and bound in China

ISBN: 978-0-8478-3863-9

Library of Congress Control Number: 2012944096

Editor: Allison Power

Project Coordinator: Matthew Kowles

Design by Doug Turshen with Steve Turner

Design Coordinator: Kayleigh Jankowski

Cover art by Charlotte Moss

I … made a menu book. I listed first courses, main cou…
the theater, Christmas dinner. I would tell my cook, 'Any of these things
One eye sees, the other feels. —Paul Klee I shut my eyes in order
things or else alone. —Ranier Maria Rilke You can only get be
faith in surfaces. A good one is full of clues. —Richard Avedon If you a
anything. —Ruth Bernhard When you live with beautiful things, you
—Ralph Rucci Notebooks are to dreams what computers are to r
go and look at everything, and then you have to ha
original. —Seaman Schepps Beauty is the prom
dance or act, though working around that minor detail made n
make variations, of course, one must begin by finding s
developed. —Valentino My rooms are 'scrapbooks' of po
Stare. It is the way to educate your eye, and more. Stare, p
have a bit of tradition. I believe in history. —Alexa
Your house is burning down, what do you grab? My scrapbooks full
People create their own questions because they are afraid to look straigh
you see it, don't sit looking at it walk. —Ayn Rand
and scrapbooks, memorials of many v
postcards, theatrical programmes, letters, photographs and fiction
childhood. —Cecil Beaton Last word to Maurice, her husband
on her bedroom shelf. —Colette The thing with high-tech is t